Hiking the
Poconos

Hiking the Poconos

A Guide to the Area's Best Hiking Adventures

John L. Young

GUILFORD, CONNECTICUT
HELENA, MONTANA

AN IMPRINT OF THE GLOBE PEQUOT PRESS

To buy books in quantity for corporate use
or incentives, call **(800) 962–0973**
or e-mail **premiums@GlobePequot.com**.

FALCONGUIDES®

Project manager: Julie Marsh
Text design: Nancy Freeborn
Layout artist: Maggie Peterson
Interior photos © John L. Young
Maps: Trailhead Graphics © Morris Book Publishing, LLC

Library of Congress Cataloging-in-Publication Data
Young, John L.
  Hiking the Poconos : a guide to the area's best
hiking adventures / John L. Young.
      p. cm.
  Includes index.
  ISBN 978-0-7627-4502-9
1. Hiking–Pennsylvania–Pocono Mountains–Guide-
books. 2. Pocono Mountains (Pa.)–Guidebooks.
I. Title.
  GV199.42.P42P639 2009
  796.5109748'2–dc22
                                        2008050387

Printed in the United States of America

10 9 8 7 6 5 4 3 2 1

To all the hiking club members and volunteers
who go out week after week, year after year,
and sometimes decade after decade
to maintain the hiking trails of Pennsylvania.

HELP US KEEP THIS GUIDE UP TO DATE

Every effort has been made by the author and editors to make this guide as accurate and useful as possible. However, many things can change after a guide is published—trails are rerouted, regulations change, techniques evolve, facilities come under new management, and so on.

We would appreciate your comments concerning your experiences with this guide and how you feel it could be improved and kept up to date. While we may not be able to respond to all comments and suggestions, we'll take them to heart, and we'll also make certain to share them with the author. Please send your comments and suggestions to the following address:

The Globe Pequot Press
Reader Response/Editorial Department
P.O. Box 480
Guilford, CT 06437

Or you may e-mail us at: editorial@globepequot.com

Thanks for your input, and happy trails!

Contents

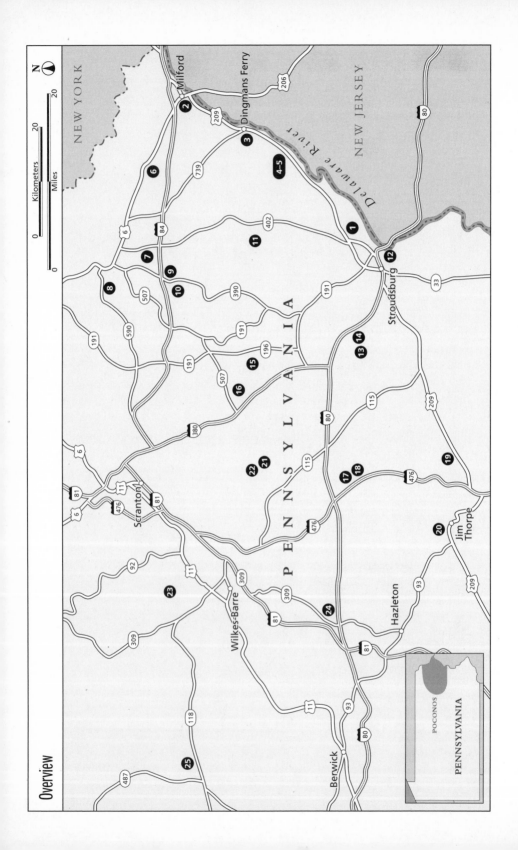

Overview

Acknowledgments

I want to thank my wife, Debra, for her support, both on and off the trail. I also want to thank my hike-mates: my brother Jim Young and his wife, Billie; Robert Bollinger; Dennis Anderson; and Keith Miller and his wife, Cindy.

From the top of Mount Minsi, you can see the Delaware River snake its way into New Jersey (hike 12).

Introduction

Hiking in the Poconos is like taking a vacation from the Real World—even if you come only for one day and one hike—it still seems as though you're on a genuine vacation. The reason for this is simple: It's different up here on the Pocono Plateau. When you drive to a hike, you drive on a two-lane highway that takes you through forests of rolling hills where you might see an abandoned resort or gas station or restaurant next to a 1950s-era getaway cabin that is next to a multimillion-dollar private residential enclave.

As for the terrain of the Poconos, its history can be traced to the last ice age, when retreating glaciers left behind hundreds of glacial lakes and dozens of wetlands and bogs. Mix with that the upheaval of the land that created deep gashes and ravines and dozens of streams that sweep through, over, around, and ultimately down the sandstone cascades, and you have a place where getting outdoors is the number-one priority.

In short, there are more glacial lakes and breathtaking waterfalls in the Poconos than any other region of Pennsylvania. This hiking guide will take you to them. You could start with Dingmans Falls, which in my mind is one of the top two or three waterfalls in the state. Before you finish this hike, you will have visited five waterfalls and walked alongside a pristine mountain stream.

Dingman Falls Visitor Center.

Want to see where the Appalachian Trail leaves the state? Hike Mount Minsi. And when you come back down, stop in the tiny village of Delaware Water Gap and have dinner in one of their two upscale restaurants, where I had one of the best meals in my travels. Besides, if you've climbed over 1,200 feet to the overlook, you deserve a reward.

The number-one attraction of the Poconos is the Delaware Water Gap National Recreation Area—a 70,000-acre recreation paradise that runs 40 miles along the Delaware River on both the Pennsylvania and the New Jersey sides and has over five million visitors a year. In 2002 the National Park Service began the McDade Trail—a 37-mile-long hiking/biking trail that runs from one end of the park to the other, mostly along the Delaware River. To date, the trail has been completed for 5 miles at its southern terminus and 4 miles at its northern terminus. These two sections are the first and second hikes in this guide.

There is much to draw hikers to the Poconos, and no place caters to hikers as does Promised Land State Park. In conjunction with the surrounding Delaware State Forest, the park manages more than 50 miles of hiking trails spread over 15,000 acres. Unique to my hiking experience in Pennsylvania, as author of *Hiking Pennsylvania,* I have never hiked a trail system that has numbered stanchions along all the hikes. In other words, once you have a park map/brochure in hand, you can see that on the Little Falls Trail in this guide, you hike from Stanchion 28 to 29; on the Bruce Lake Natural Area Trail, you begin at 55 and walk directly to 56; and so on for the entire hike. And the map itself is without question the nicest park map in the state park system.

There are two hikes in Big Pocono State Park. One takes you to an overlook on Camelback Mountain that many hikers claim gives the best view in the Poconos. The other takes you to a swamp that may be the most picturesque swamp hikers will see anywhere. From there it's on to a perfectly round glacial lake, another ice-age remnant.

Speaking of the last ice age, one hike in this guide leads you to the boulder field in Hickory Run State Park. As you will learn when you visit the educational kiosk, the boulders that lie in this perfectly flat field are the result of a moraine, also the result of glacial retreat. Except in this instance, over time and cyclical freezing and thawing, the boulders slid down the moraine to form this mysterious boulder field.

There are a number of hikes in state forests. Two of these hikes, Choke Creek and Big Pine Hill, are located in areas so pretty that hikers should bring a camera. And the forest at Big Pine Hill, replete with abandoned white-pine plantations, is so inviting that even the parking area looks like a park.

I have made my circle of the Poconos large so that this guide includes hikes that are a little farther away from the center of the area. The reason for this is simple: These outlying hikes are well worth visiting. I take readers to the village of Jim Thorpe to hike the Glen Onoko Falls Trail and walk the rugged path alongside the stream to view a number of breathtaking waterfalls that are, aside from everything else, just plain beautiful.

From Jim Thorpe it's a short drive to Beltzville State Park, where I lead you to Wild Creek Falls, which is altogether different from Glen Onoko: Here a meandering stream flows over flat boulders and creates waterfalls and deep, clear pools where children wade, dogs swim out to fetch sticks, and families eat lunch on a giant boulder with their toes dangling in the water.

Nescopeck and Frances Slocum State Parks are near the Willes-Barre-Scranton corridor, and each merits a visit. At Nescopeck the trail winds along the magnificent Nescopeck Creek then alongside ponds, swamps, and Lake Frances. Along the way you can visit the newly constructed park office and dam. At Frances Slocum State Park, the hike leads you through a netherworld of stone fences that were built over one hundred years ago to set boundaries and, in some cases, to fence in livestock.

Finally, I included Ricketts Glen—in my opinion, the number-one hike in the state. It consists of twenty-two named waterfalls and a man-made walkway—the Falls Trail—that takes you up one side and down the other of a stream that plummets 1,000 feet down the face of the Allegheny Front. Ricketts is not only a great hike but also one of the most photographed sites in the state.

Pocono Weather

Beginning in the second half of the nineteenth century, workers who once lived and worked on farms began migrating to the major industrial areas of the East to work

One of the many falls along the Little Falls Trail.

in the factories that were to spearhead the country's Industrial Revolution. These factories, originally powered by streams and rivers, were located in low-lying areas that experienced sweltering summers with high humidity and temperatures that ran to the 90s and even over 100 degrees.

It was during this era that mountain regions in Pennsylvania began attracting tourists by promoting their cool mountain air. These early resort owners were onto something. In northeast Pennsylvania and regions like the Pocono Plateau, which sits 1,000 to 1,500 feet higher than the surrounding lowlands, summer temperatures are 5 to 10 degrees lower than their lowland neighbors.

Typically, summer daytime temperatures run 70 to 80 degrees and the nights drop to the 50s and 60s. In the months of July and August, there is on average just one day each month when temperatures reach 90 degrees. There is only one recorded instance, in 1911, when the temperature reached 100 degrees.

These higher elevations also ensure that the Poconos receive 8 to 12 inches more rain than lower elevations do. In June, July, and August, there is an average of eight thunderstorms each month. But these storms are of short duration. In winter the Poconos get 10 to 20 inches more snow than the lower areas. Total snowfall reaches 50 to 60 inches, making it a paradise for winter activities, especially downhill and cross-country skiing.

One theory of the extensive stone walls in this area is that early farmers built them to contain livestock (hike 23).

The long and the short of it is that the Poconos just might have the most pleasant climate in the state. Hiking the area from April to October, I didn't lose one day to rain. Even when it did rain, it was of a short duration, and I was still able to hike that day.

Flora and Fauna

The Nature Conservancy has included the Pocono Plateau on its list of the "Last Great Places," and once you start hiking around, you'll understand why. The Poconos are home to most of the predominant flora across the state. But because it is a glaciated plateau and its terrain is dotted with glacial lakes, boreal wetlands and forests, heath lands, swamps, and bogs, it is also home to a number of rare and exotic species of plants that thrive on the plateau and on into the northern regions, such as Canada.

As for trees, there is the ubiquitous hemlock, which not only clings to the slopes of riparian ravines but also can be found in and around the area's many bogs, along with the tamarack, black tupelo, gray birch, red spruce, quaking and bigtooth aspen, and balsam firs—some 80 feet tall. The hardwood forest on the plateau is much the same as it is across the state, with the dominant species being oak, maple, beech, birch, and black cherry.

There is a diversity of plant life here unlike any other region of the state. The many swamps and bogs provide a providential habitat for unusual insect-eating plants like the sundew and pitcher plant. But just like most of the rest of the state, the Poconos are home to many ordinary, everyday wildflowers such as knapweed, bull thistle, Queen Anne's lace, star flower, mountain bluets (also known as Quaker ladies), sheep laurel, joe-pye weed, mountain laurel, and azaleas. In fact, one species of azalea in the Poconos—the rhodora—is quite famous.

The great American thinker Ralph Waldo Emerson was so smitten with the rhodora that he wrote a poem about it titled, as you might guess, "The Rhodora." To celebrate this member of the heath family, each spring The Nature Conservancy of the Poconos invites photographers from all over the world to visit its preserve at Long Pond in Blakeslee to photograph this deciduous shrub when its magenta flowers bloom.

Because of the unique and sometimes rare bushes and shrubs that thrive here, the Pocono Plateau also is home to a number of rare moths, butterflies, and birds. In fact, the Audubon Society lists the Poconos as one of its Important Bird Areas of Pennsylvania. Here you may see the American bittern, northern harrier, Blackburnian warbler, Canada warbler, and eastern wood-pewee. And how about this name for a rare moth endemic to the Poconos: the fly-poison bulb-borer moth.

There are more than sixty species of mammals in Pennsylvania, and most of them are here on the plateau—from the tiny pygmy shrew to the white-tailed deer to a 500-pound black bear. Hikers may not see beavers, but if you are hiking near water, chances are you'll see a beaver dam. You may even see a native river otter, which have been wiped out in many other sections of the state and recently reintroduced here.

Black bears are alive and well in the Poconos. One reason the black bears thrive here is that the many swamps and bogs protect bears from hunters. The bears retreat to the swampy bogs where hunters can't follow. In addition, many shrubs and bushes and the hardwood forests provide berries, acorns, and beechnuts for the bears' diet.

Having hiked from one end of the state to the other over the past decade, I have had only two bear sightings. In each case it was a mother bear with one to three cubs moving away from me on all fours. I relate this to emphasize that the black bears of Pennsylvania are not interested in interacting with hikers. If you are concerned about meeting a black bear in the woods, always hike in a group. Bears are less likely to confront a group simply because they feel it would be more difficult to get something from a group of adversaries than a lone hiker.

Wilderness Restrictions/Regulations

Ten of the twenty-five hikes in this book are in state parks. Six are on federal land, namely the Delaware Water Gap National Recreation Area. Five hikes are in state forests. Three are on state game lands, and one is on private land owned by Pennsylvania Power & Light. There are no fees or restrictions for hiking on these properties.

The biggest landholder on the Pocono Plateau is the state game lands—120,000 acres when you combine all its numbered parcels. Delaware State Forest is second,

The Glen Onoko Falls hike (hike 20) begins on a road once used to access the local hotel.

with 82,000 acres. Next is the Delaware Water Gap National Recreation Area, with 67,000 acres. The combined total of ten state parks is more than 40,000 acres, and Pennsylvania Power & Light owns 5,700-acre Lake Wallenpaupack along with 13 miles of its shoreline.

None of these agencies, which own land across the Commonwealth, have any hiking restrictions, nor do any of them charge a use fee. This makes Pennsylvania an excellent state in which to hike, and one could certainly add that the Poconos are at the top of the list for places not only to hike but also to get away from civilization and get a feel for what Mother Nature is all about. The Poconos truly are one of the Last Great Places.

How to Use This Guide

This guidebook contains everything you'll need to choose, plan, and enjoy a hike in the Poconos. Stuffed with Pocono-specific information, *Hiking the Poconos* features twenty-five mapped and cued hikes as well as everything from advice on getting into shape to tips on getting the most out of hiking with your children or your dog. And as you'd expect with any FalconGuide, you get the best maps man and technology can render. We've done everything but load your pack and lace up your boots. With so much information, the only question you may have is: How do I sift through it all? Well, we answer that, too.

Kayaking on the Delaware River.

We've designed our FalconGuide to be highly visual, for quick reference and ease of use. You don't have to waste time poring through bulky hike descriptions to get mileage cues or elevation stats. They're set out for you. Take the time to dive into a hike description and you'll realize that this guide is not just a good source of information; it's also a good read. In the end you get the best of both worlds: a quick-reference guide and an engaging look at a region. Here's an outline of the guide's major components.

What You'll Find in a FalconGuide

Let's start with the individual chapter. To aid in quick decision-making, we start each chapter with a short overview that gives you a taste of the hiking adventure at hand. You'll learn about the trail terrain and what surprises the route has to offer. If your interest is piqued, you can read more. If not, skip to the next hike.

The hike specs are fairly self-explanatory. Here you'll find the quick, nitty-gritty details of the hike: where the trailhead is located, the county and nearest town, hike distance and type (out-and-back, loop, or lollipop), approximate hiking time, difficulty rating, trail terrain, what other trail users you may encounter, fees or permits required, and the park or trail schedule.

Trail contacts provides the Web site and direct phone number for the local land managers in charge of all the trails within the selected hike. Use this hotline to call ahead for trail access information.

Maps suggests other maps to supplement the maps in this book. They are listed in order from most detailed to most general.

Finding the trailhead gives you dependable directions from a nearby interstate highway or city right down to where you'll want to park.

The Hike is the meat of the chapter. Detailed and honest, it's the author's carefully researched impression of the trail. While it's impossible to cover everything, you can rest assured that we won't miss what's important.

Miles and Directions provides mileage cues to identify all turns and trail name changes, as well as points of interest.

Hike Information is a hodgepodge of information, including area or town visitor bureaus and local outdoor retailers (for emergency trail supplies). We'll also suggest where to stay, where to eat, and what else to see and do while you're hiking in the area. Any other important or useful information will also be listed here such as local attractions, outdoor shops, nearby accommodations, etc.

How to Use the Maps

We don't want anyone to feel restricted to just the routes and trails that are mapped here. We hope you will have an adventurous spirit and use this guide as a platform to explore the Poconos and discover new routes for yourself. One of the simplest ways to do this is to just turn the map upside down and hike the trail in reverse. The change in perspective is fantastic, and the hike should feel quite different. It will be like getting two distinctly different hikes on each map.

You may wish to copy the directions for the trail onto a small sheet to help you while hiking. Or just slip the whole book into your pack and take it with you. Enjoy your time in the outdoors—and remember to pack out what you pack in.

State Overview

This map (page viii) helps you find your way to the start of each hike from the nearest sizable town or city. Coupled with the detailed directions at the beginning of each hike, this map should visually lead you to the trailhead.

Route Map

This is your primary guide to each hike. It shows all the accessible roads and trails, points of interest, water, towns, landmarks, and geographical features. It also distinguishes trails from roads and paved roads from unpaved roads. The selected route is highlighted, and directional arrows point the way.

Trail Finder Chart

Number	Hike	Waterfalls	With Children	For Backpackers	Great Views	Peak Baggers	Geology Lovers	Lake Lovers	Nature Lovers
1	McDade Trail South		●						
2	McDade Trail North		●						
3	Dingmans Falls	●					●		
4	Ridgeline Trail						●		●
5	Tumbling Waters Trail	●			●				●
6	Shohola Falls	●						●	●
7	Blooming Grove Trail								●
8	Shuman Point Natural Area		●					●	●
9	Bruce Lake Natural Area			●				●	●
10	Little Falls Trail		●						
11	Pennel Run			●			●		●
12	Mount Minsi			●	●	●	●		
13	Wolf Swamp and Deep Lake						●	●	●

Trail Finder Chart

Number	Hike	Waterfalls	With Children	For Backpackers	Great Views	Peak Baggers	Geology Lovers	Lake Lovers	Nature Lovers
14	Big Pocono State Park				•	•	•		
15	Tobyhanna State Park		•					•	
16	Gouldsboro State Park						•	•	
17	Hickory Run Boulder Field		•				•		
18	Hawk Falls	•	•						
19	Beltzville State Park	•	•					•	
20	Glen Onoko Falls Trail	•			•	•	•		
21	Choke Creek Trail			•					•
22	Big Pine Hill			•	•				•
23	Frances Slocum State Park		•					•	•
24	Nescopeck State Park		•					•	•
25	Ricketts Glen	•					•		•

Map Legend

Transportation

Interstate Highway	═══⟨15⟩═══
U.S. Highway	═══⟨27⟩═══
State Road	═══⟨19⟩═══
County/Forest Road	═⟨250⟩═⟨FR 13⟩═
Dirt Road	= = = = =
Railroad	┝━┿━┿━┥
Featured Trail	▬▬▬▬▬
Other Trail	- - - - - -
Direction of travel	→
Turnaround	↺

Hydrology

Lake/Reservoir	⬤
River/Creek	～～
Marsh/Swamp	⸺⸺
Waterfall	⫽

Political

State border	- - - - - -

Symbols

Campground	▲
Point of Interest	■
Mountain/Peak	▲
Parking	🅿
Picnic Area	⊞
Restroom	⊞
Tower	⍗
City/Town	○
Trailhead (Start)	❺
Bridge	≍
Boat launch	⬳
Gate	•—•
Viewpoint	✦
Steps	⦀⦀

Land Use

National Park	▭
State Park	▭

True North
(Magnetic North is
approximately 15.5° East) N ⬆

1 McDade Trail South

This section of the McDade Trail was opened in 2002 and takes you right alongside the Delaware River.

Get ready for some great views of the Delaware River on this easy, mostly flat hike as you walk on a wide trail of crushed rock. Along the way, you pass through a pine plantation, open fields, and a typical broadleaf forest.

Start: Turn Farm trailhead parking area on River Road

County: Monroe

Nearest town: East Stroudsburg

Distance: 10.6 miles out and back or 5.3-mile shuttle

Approximate hiking time: 4 hours (2 hours for shuttle)

Difficulty rating: Easy

Terrain: Wide, crushed-rock trail

Elevation gain: 100 feet

Land status: National recreation area

Other trail users: Hunters (in season), bicyclists, cross-country skiers

Canine compatibility: Pets not permitted in summer

Fees/permits: No fees or permits required

Schedule: Year-round; caution advised during hunting seasons

Trail contacts: Delaware Water Gap National Recreation Area, Bushkill; (570) 426-2435; www.nps.gov/dewa

Maps: USGS: Bushkill; Delaware Water Gap National Recreation Area map and brochure

McDade Trail South

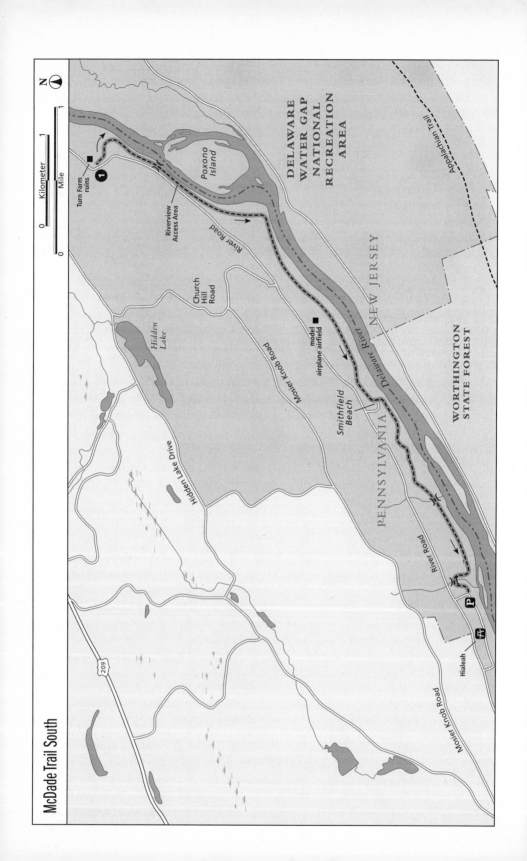

Finding the trailhead: From New Jersey cross the Interstate 80 bridge and take exit 310 (the first Pennsylvania exit), following the signs to the Pennsylvania Welcome Center. At the welcome center set your odometer to 0.0 and drive north on River Road for 8.0 miles to the Turn Farm parking area on your right. *DeLorme: Pennsylvania Atlas & Gazetteer:* Page 54 D3

The Hike

The McDade Trail is one of the newest trails in the Poconos. It is also a work in progress. When completed it will stretch along the Delaware River for a total of 37 miles, from Hialeah Beach at the southern end to Milford Beach at the northern terminus. Our hike is the 5.0-mile section from the Turn Farm on River Road south to Hialeah Beach. This section, which opened in 2002, was the first section to be completed.

The land along the river here started out as farmland, the same as much of the land in the area. After a devastating flood in 1955, the federal government came up with a plan to build a dam at Docks Island to eliminate the chance of more flooding and create a recreation area around the resultant reservoir. The government bought up all the land along the river, and the farms and settlements were for the most part demolished. But after decades of bitter argument, the dam was abandoned and the government turned the area into the Delaware Water Gap National Recreation Area.

Some of those early buildings remain, but most of them are gone—victims of arson, the wrecking crew, or the ravages of time. At the John Turn Farm trailhead, you can see the remains of a foundation and the ruins of a few stone outbuildings.

To start this hike, walk to the right of the foundation to a yellow stanchion. From there it's downhill with River Road to your right, then a sharp turn to set you walking downstream. You are sharing this trail with bicyclists so, as is customary on bike trails, it's best to stay to the far right.

There are a number of access points to the river along this trail. The first one you reach is called Riverview. It's a parking lot with a gate across the road that leads out to River Road. Before the trail was built, you could drive into the parking area; but the gate now prohibits vehicles from accessing the trail. From the parking area paths lead down to the river's edge, where you can cast your fishing line, snap a photo, or just enjoy an unobstructed view of the river as it meanders on its way to Chesapeake Bay.

At 3.0 miles arrive at Smithfield Beach, where you walk past the bathhouse and walk on the sidewalk past the restrooms at the southern end of the beach. Continue past the restrooms to the woods, where the trail continues.

This easy hike passes through a broadleaf forest, so for the most part you are hiking in the shade. At other times you walk through magnificent pine forests or farmers' fields. If you want to see the Delaware River up close and want to spend a day in a pristine forest, making your way from one access point to the next, this hike is definitely for you.

If you have a second vehicle, someone to pick you up, or another ingenious way to accomplish it, you can do this hike as a shuttle. If you have new or older hikers and just want to hike a portion of the trail then return to your vehicle, start at the Turn

Farm trailhead. There is only one serious climb, and it is at the very beginning of the northbound hike out of the Hialeah trailhead.

Miles and Directions

0.0 Start at the Turn Farm parking area and walk toward the trail, which begins on the right side of the old foundation and is marked with a yellow stanchion. The trail goes downhill.

0.2 Come to a Sᴛᴇᴇᴘ Hɪʟʟ sign and a steep descent.

0.3 The trail turns right. You are now walking downstream, with the Delaware River on your left.

0.6 Pass a gate on your right and a fisherman's path to the river. There are foundation ruins on your left next to the path.

0.7 Cross a ravine on a footbridge.

0.9 Pass through the Riverview Access Area parking lot.

1.2 The trail leaves the woods and you walk alongside a farmer's field.

1.4 Get your first view of Poxono Island.

1.7 Pass a fisherman's path to the river.

2.2 Pass the Roxbury Model Airplane Club grounds on your right.

3.0 Arrive at Smithfield Beach. Walk past the main bathhouse and past the restrooms to the woods, where you pick up the trail.

3.7 Pass a farmer's field.

4.0 The trail turns right then jogs left. Stay on the crushed-rock trail. Ignore the path that goes straight toward River Road.

4.3 Cross a ravine on a second footbridge.

4.8 Climb a steep hill.

5.1 Cross a third footbridge over a ravine.

5.2 Climb a steep ascent.

5.3 Reach the Hialeah trailhead. If you don't have a shuttle vehicle, retrace your steps.

10.6 Arrive back at the Turn Farm parking area.

Hike Information

Local Information
Pocono Mountains Visitors Bureau: 1004 Main Street, Stroudsburg; (570) 421-5791 or (800) 762-6667 (570); www.800poconos.com

Local Events/Attractions
Antoine Dutot Museum and Gallery: Main Street, Delaware Water Gap; (570) 476-4240; www.dutotmuseum.com

Shawnee Playhouse: Five River Road, Shawnee-on-Delaware; (570) 421-5093; www.theshawneeplayhouse.com

Accommodations
Gatehouse Country Inn: River Road, Shawnee-on-Delaware; (570) 420-4553; www.gatehousecountryinn.com

Delaware Water Gap KOA: 233 Hollow Road, East Stroudsburg; (570) 223-8000; www.delaware watergapkoa.com

Restaurants
Pizzaros Pizzeria: Fox Run Plaza, Marshalls Creek; (570) 223-1888
Shawnee General Store: River Road, Shawnee-on-Delaware; (570) 421-0956

Organizations
Pocono Outdoor Club: www.poconooutdoorclub.org

Local Outdoor Retailers
Dunkleberger's Sports Outfitters: 585 Main Street, Stroudsburg; (570) 421-7950
Wal-Mart: 355 Lincoln Avenue, East Stroudsburg; (570) 424-8415

WELCOME TO PENNSYLVANIA: THE INTERSTATE 80 WELCOME CENTER

If you're a brochure junkie like me, the first thing you want to do when you hit a new area is go right to the source of all the colorful pamphlets, maps, and assorted freebies. If you're coming to the Poconos on I-80 from the New Jersey side of the Delaware River, you won't have far to go: The new welcome center at Delaware Water Gap on I-80 is your first exit (exit 310). If you're coming from the west on I-80, exit 310 is the last Pennsylvania exit. In either case, take the exit and follow the sign.

The 12,700-square-foot center opened in May 2006 at a cost of $9.9 million. The Pennsylvania Historical Commission has installed four exhibits that showcase the area's history in regard to the Poconos, Native American history and footpaths, William Penn and Ben Franklin, and the Pennsylvania Trails of History.

The building, which is faced with granite squares and supported by columns installed on the open center court of concrete squares, has a wheelchair-accessible rooftop garden and a grassy area with picnic tables.

The center is open 24/7 and is staffed from 7:00 a.m. to 7:00 p.m. daily. For more information call (570) 234-1180.

2 McDade Trail North

The wide trail is made of crushed stone and is open to road and mountain bikers and cross-country skiers.

Like the McDade Trail South, this hike is easy going and provides up-close views of the Delaware River, which is more than 20 feet deep at some spots. You begin at historic Milford Beach, where you can photograph the river and, if you're lucky, get a shot of kayakers as they navigate downstream. You will also see where the Pocono Plateau ends and visit the experimental Pittman Orchard.

Start: Milford Beach parking area
County: Pike
Nearest town: Milford
Distance: 5.0 miles out and back
Approximate hiking time: 2 hours
Difficulty rating: Easy
Terrain: Wide, crushed-rock trail
Elevation gain: 120 feet
Land status: National recreation area
Other trail users: Hunters (in season), bicyclists, cross-country skiers

Canine compatibility: Pets not permitted in summer
Fees/permits: No fees or permits required
Schedule: Year-round; caution advised during hunting seasons
Trail contacts: Delaware Water Gap National Recreation Area, Bushkill; (570) 426-2435; www.nps.gov/dewa
Maps: USGS: Milford; Delaware Water Gap National Recreation Area map and brochure

Finding the trailhead: From New Jersey cross the Interstate 80 bridge and take exit 309 to U.S. Route 209. Follow US 209 north for 4 miles to the intersection of U.S. Business 209 and US 209. Turn right at the intersection to stay on US 209. Drive north on US 209 for 27 miles, and turn right at the sign for Milford Beach. Turn right at the stoplight; continue into Milford Beach, and turn right into the parking area. Park just south of the middle of the lot. *DeLorme: Pennsylvania Atlas & Gazetteer:* Page 55 B5

The Hike

As soon as you park your vehicle in the parking lot at Milford Beach, you realize that this hike provides some of the best views of the Delaware River in the Poconos. The only way to get any closer to the river would be in a kayak or a canoe.

Milford Beach started out as the Blood Family Farm, but the family abandoned farming because of perennial flooding. In 1945 Robert Blood took over the land and created a beach resort with picnic pavilions, a snack bar, a diving float, and even boats for hire. The enterprise soon became known as Bob's Beach. In the 1980s the National Park Service purchased the land and developed it into the beach we see today.

After you walk to the beach for photos or just to take in the view, walk west past your vehicle toward the tree line and the beginning of a split-rail fence. A yellow stanchion here marks the beginning of the trail.

In 0.2 mile you are under the U.S. 206 bridge. If you've ever wanted to see or photograph the underside of a bridge, this is your chance. From this low, river's edge point, make a short climb onto a plateau and into a hemlock forest. At about 1.0 mile you notice a clearing to your right and a lot of tree stumps bulldozed up alongside the trail. This is the site of the old Milford dump.

At about 1.5 miles—if you happen to be there at the right time on the right day— you will hear a whining sound overhead. This would be the remote-controlled planes of the Flying Hawks maneuvering overhead in dips, wide arcs, and dive-bombing modes. Their airfield is to your right, closer to US 209.

Also along this stretch you will see on your right a spectacular cliff rising 500 feet above the ground. This is the end of the Poconos, literally. This picturesque cliff— actually, an eroded ridge—that stretches 3 miles south from the town of Milford is the eastern fringe of the Pocono Plateau. The Buchanan family, who had owned the land atop the ridge since 1803, opened the Cliff Park Inn in 1900. "The Cliff" was sold to the Conservation Fund in 2002, which continues to run the inn.

During the early years of moviemaking, The Cliff was chosen as the filming site of the 1912 silent movie *The Informer,* starring Mary Pickford. In the 1920s and 1930s, a number of Western movies starring Pennsylvania's very own cowboy, Tom Mix, were filmed here.

At 2.3 miles you leave the open field and enter a forest of old, arthritic-looking trees. You are entering Pittman Orchard, which was a going concern in the 1930s but today is little more than a testimony to the tenacity of trees to continue standing

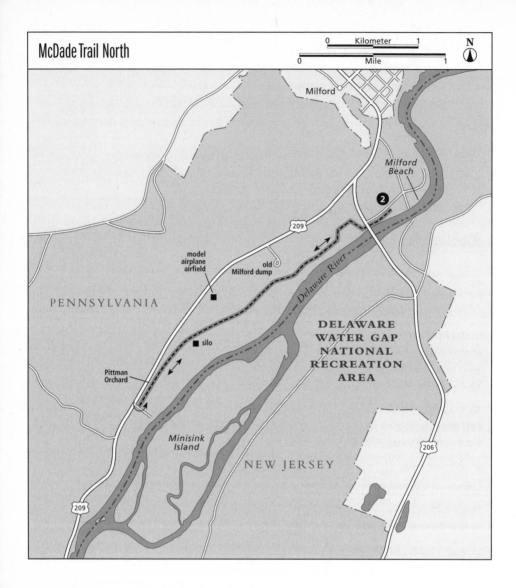

long after they are dead. The trail—that is, this hike—ends at the southern end of the orchard, where there is a gate across a washed-out access road that runs out to US 209. This is the end of the line, so retrace your steps back to Milford Beach.

Miles and Directions

0.0   Start at the parking area and walk to the yellow stanchion at the beginning of the split-rail fence near the woods.

0.2   Pass under the US 206 bridge across the Delaware River.

0.3 The trail turns right and you begin an uphill climb into the forest.

0.4 Ignore an access road on your right.

0.5 Enter a hemlock forest.

1.0 Pass the old Milford dump on your right.

1.5 Pass the Flying Hawks remote-controlled model airplane airfield.

1.9 Arrive at an intersection with a road that runs from US 209 on your right to the silo on your left. Continue straight.

2.3 Arrive at the northern edge of Pittman Orchard. Note the old apple trees.

2.5 Arrive at the end of the trail. There is a gate across an access road that goes right to US 209. Retrace your steps back to the Milford Beach parking area.

5.0 Arrive back at your vehicle.

Hike Information

Local Information

Pocono Mountains Visitors Bureau: 1004 Main Street, Stroudsburg; (570) 421-5791 or (800) 762-6667; www.800poconos.com

Local Events/Attractions

Annual Classic Car Show: May, Pocmont Resort, Bushkill; (570) 588-6671 or (800) 762-6668; www.pocmont.com
Pocono Indian Museum: Bushkill; (570) 588-9338

Accommodations

Cliff Park Inn: Milford; (570) 296-6491 or (800) 225-6535; www.cliffparkinn.com
Outdoor World Campgrounds: Bushkill; (800) 222-5557

Restaurants

Seasons Restaurant at Pocmont Resort: Bushkill Falls Road, Bushkill; (800) 762-6668

Organizations

Pocono Outdoor Club: www.poconooutdoorclub.org

Local Outdoor Retailers

Delaware River Discovery Center: road and mountain bike rentals, Shawnee-on-Delaware; (877) 373-2386
Pike County Outfitters: Apple Valley Village, U.S. Route 6, Milford; (570) 296-9492; www.pike countyoutfitters.net/index.htm
Starting Gate Action Sports: road and mountain bike rentals, Marshalls Creek; (570) 223-6215
Wal-Mart: U.S. Routes 6/209, Milford; (570) 491-4940

ZANE GREY MUSEUM

Zane Grey was one of the twentieth century's most prolific and popular writers. His primary genre was the adult Western. His most noted Western, *Riders of the Purple Sage,* came out in 1912 and was an instant success. Grey's success continued through the Great Depression in the 1930s, when he became involved in the movie industry in Hollywood. A number of his books were made into Western films.

Grey met his wife, Dolly, while canoeing on the Delaware River in Lackawaxen. In fact, Grey's first published article was "A Day on the Delaware," published by *Recreation* magazine in 1902. Grey also wrote about his expeditions to the American West and his fishing exploits around the world. At one time Grey held more than ten world records for large game fish. He was the first person to catch a fish over 1,000 pounds—a blue marlin—with a rod and reel.

In 1914 he and his wife purchased the house that is now the museum as a summer residence. The Greys also had homes on Catalina Island and in Arizona and Oregon, plus fishing camps in New Zealand, Australia, and Tahiti.

Grey died in 1939, and in 1945 his widow sold their summer home in Lackawaxen to friends who turned it into the Zane Grey Inn. The inn operated until 1973, when the new owners turned the house into a museum to showcase Grey's memorabilia, photographs, and books. In 1989 the National Park Service bought the museum and it became part of the Upper Delaware Scenic and Recreational River.

For more information call (570) 729-8251.

3 Dingmans Falls

A wheelchair-accessible walkway ensures that every visitor can get up close to Dingmans Falls, one of the most dramatic waterfalls in the state.

Dingmans Falls is one of the top three waterfalls in Pennsylvania. This hike takes you to the falls and then through a hemlock forest alongside a pristine stream to three more waterfalls and the ruins of a once-thriving mill.

Start: Dingmans Falls Visitor Center parking lot
County: Pike
Nearest town: Milford
Distance: 5.0 miles out and back
Approximate hiking time: 3 hours
Difficulty rating: Easy; mostly level trail, with a short climb out of a ravine
Terrain: Wooden walkways, wooden steps, pine needle–covered paths
Elevation gain: 558 feet

Land status: National recreation area
Other trail users: Tourists
Canine compatibility: Leashed dogs permitted
Fees/permits: No fees or permits required
Schedule: Year-round
Trail contacts: Delaware Water Gap National Recreation Area, Bushkill Falls; (570) 426-2435; www.nps.gov/dewa
Maps: USGS: Lake Maskenozha

Finding the trailhead: From Wilkes-Barre drive south on Interstate 476 and get on Interstate 80 heading east toward Stroudsburg. From I-80 take exit 309 in Stroudsburg and drive north on

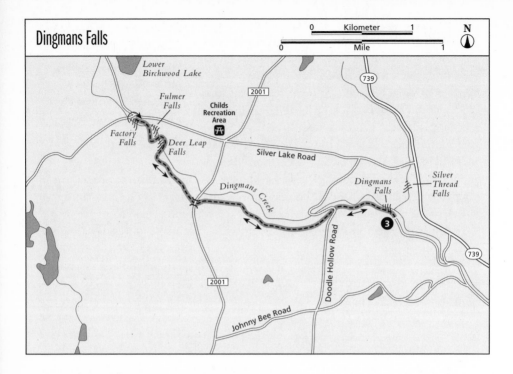

Dingmans Falls

U.S. Route 209 for 4 miles to the intersection of U.S. Business 209 and US 209. Turn right at the stoplight to stay on US 209, and drive north for 20 miles. Turn left onto Johnny Bee Road and then turn right at the sign for Dingmans Falls. *DeLorme: Pennsylvania Atlas & Gazetteer:* Page 55 C5

The Hike

This hike is located within the Delaware Water Gap National Recreation Area, a 70,000-acre watershed that stretches for 40 miles on both the Pennsylvania and New Jersey sides of the Delaware River. The trail begins on a wooden walkway that takes you to the foot of Silver Thread Falls, where water from a tributary to Dingmans Creek drops 80 feet through a narrow shale crevasse, cascading over a series of ledges.

The walkway leads to a viewing platform at the base of Dingmans Falls, where rushing waters leap from one shale ledge to the next, creating a dramatic 130-foot drop. From the viewing platform, steps take you to a higher viewing ledge, then onto a rock outcrop above the falls. For nonhikers this is the end of the tour. There are three more falls to visit; nonhikers can return to their cars and drive to the upper falls area.

Our hike continues with a short climb into the forest on a well-worn, root-covered path beside the rock outcrop above Dingmans Falls. From this point the trail essentially follows the creek through a hemlock ravine for 2 miles to our destination, the George Childs Recreation Area.

As you walk through the ravine, it's easy to see why the eastern hemlock is Pennsylvania's state tree. With its shallow root system, the hemlock can grow just about anywhere, but it thrives in damp ravines. Native Americans and early European settlers ground hemlock bark into a powder that was used to stop bleeding. They made tea from hemlock bark and used it as a remedy for sore gums and other ailments. Tannin from the hemlock bark was also used in tanning leather.

Many lifelong outdoors enthusiasts have never seen a black bear in the wild, but black bears are alive and well in the Delaware Water Gap National Recreation Area. These opportunistic feeders—who are primarily nocturnal—tend to raid campers' and picnickers' food stashes and garbage. Most black bears are black with a tan muzzle and a white mark on their chests; a few are cinnamon colored.

▶ **Pike County is named for General Zebulun Pike, the first white man to explore the 14,110-foot peak in the Colorado Rockies that became known as "Pikes Peak."**

Adult black bears in Pennsylvania are anywhere from 50 to 85 inches long and stand about 30 inches at the shoulder. Weights for adults range from 140 to 400 pounds, with rare individuals weighing as much as 800 pounds. Here in Pike County, a record-setting adult male weighing 864 pounds was taken in 2003.

Statewide, the black bear population has risen steadily: In 1970 there were approximately 4,000 bears in Pennsylvania; in 2007 the population was estimated to be between 14,000 and 15,000. To control the population, there's a three-day hunting season monitored by the Pennsylvania Game Commission in late November.

The trail along this section is a pleasant stroll through open woods. At times you'll have to climb out of the ravine, away from the stream, but these jaunts are short. Most of the time you walk beside the creek until you reach the Childs Recreation Area, where once again you'll find yourself in a somewhat touristy area. A network of walkways and wooden steps, complete with viewing platforms, lead from the parking lot to the picnic area and to the falls.

There are three waterfalls here: Deer Leap, Fulmer, and Factory—one right above the other and each uniquely different from the others. There's also a stone ruin, a reminder that the waters from Dingmans Creek have run a number of mills throughout the years.

Miles and Directions

0.0 Start at the gravel path from the parking lot, and walk past the information booth. Cross Dingmans Creek on a wooden footbridge, and continue on the wooden walkway to Silver Thread Falls.

0.2 Stay on the walkway. Cross Dingmans Creek on a second bridge.

0.3 Arrive at Dingmans Falls. Walk to the viewing platform. Retrace your steps and turn right onto the wooden steps.

0.5 Cross Dingmans Creek on a wooden bridge.

0.6 Arrive at the fenced viewing area and educational plaque above Dingmans Falls. The walkway for this section ends. (**Option:** Nonhikers can turn around here.) Turn left onto a worn path and climb uphill over the roots. Enter a forest of hemlock and rhododendron.

0.7 Cross Doodle Hollow Road. Note the blocked bridge on your right. Continue on the south side of the creek.

1.4 An abandoned railroad grade comes in from your left and merges with the trail. The trail turns right.

1.6 Cross State Route 2001 (paved).

1.7 The trail becomes an abandoned logging road. Turn right onto an earthen mound and walk to the creek. Turn left at the creek.

2.0 Cross a pipeline swath.

2.1 Cross a wooden bridge over Dingmans Creek and arrive at Deer Leap Falls. Walk through the picnic area and turn left onto the wooden steps.

2.2 Pass a set of steps on your right. Turn left onto a bridge above Deer Leap Falls.

2.3 Turn right onto the wooden walkway.

2.4 Cross the creek on a wooden bridge at Fulmer Falls. Turn left and walk through the picnic area to Factory Falls.

2.5 Arrive at Factory Falls. View the falls and retrace your steps.

5.0 Arrive back at the parking lot and your vehicle.

Hike Information

Local Information
Pocono Mountains Visitors Bureau: 1004 Main Street, Stroudsburg; (570) 421-5791 or (800) 762-6667; www.800poconos.com

Local Events/Attractions
Bushkill Falls: Bushkill Falls Road, Bushkill; (570) 588–6682 or (888) 628-7454); www.visitbush killfalls.com
Delaware State Forest: more than 30 miles of mountain biking trails; Swiftwater; (570) 895-4000

Accommodations
Black Walnut Country Inn: 179 Fire Tower Road, Milford; (570) 296-6322; www.theblackwalnut inn.com
Ken's Woods Campground: Bushkill; (570) 588-6381

Restaurants
Waterwheel Cafe & Bakery: The Upper Mill, 150 Water Street, Milford; (570) 296-2383; www .waterwheelcafe.com

Organizations
Pocono Outdoor Club: www.poconooutdoorclub.org

Local Outdoor Retailers
Pike County Outfitters: Apple Valley Village, U.S. Route 6, Milford; (570) 296-9492; www.pikecounty outfitters.net
Wal-Mart: U.S. Routes 6/209, Milford; (570) 491-4940

In Addition

Dingmans Ferry and Dingmans Bridge

The history of Dingmans Bridge begins in the mid-1600s when Dutch farmers settled the rich river-bottom land on both the New Jersey and the Pennsylvania sides of the Delaware River. In 1735 farmer Andreas Dingman decided he'd relocate from the New Jersey to the Pennsylvania side. To facilitate his move, he built a flatboat to cross to his new land—which he called Dingmans Choice. Soon the enterprising Dingman began ferrying people across the river on his flatboat, charging a small fee.

Dingman, and then his descendants, operated the ferry until 1836, when the Dingmans Choice and Delaware Bridge Company built their first bridge across the Delaware River. In 1803 Judge Daniel Dingman built the stone Ferry House, which still stands today beside the bridge.

This first bridge, which was made of little more than wooden planks resting on pilings in the riverbed, lasted until 1847, when high waters washed away a bridge upstream in Milford and the debris crashed into Dingmans Bridge. The bridge was destroyed and washed downstream, taking with it 200 passenger pigeons owned by Andrew Dingman III that had roosted on the bridge.

Dingmans Bridge reflected in the Delaware River.

The ferry was brought back into service for the next three years until a second bridge was completed in 1863. Just thirteen years later, tragedy struck again as high winds toppled the bridge over and sent it floating down the river. By this time you've got to imagine that the Dingmans had about had it with bridges. Once again the ferry was brought back into service—this time for thirty-seven years.

Meanwhile, in 1868 the U.S. Postal Service decided that the village of Dingmans Choice was doing so well that it needed its own post office. But there was a hitch: Some Postal Service officials thought that Dingmans Choice was not a good name for the village, so they renamed it Dingmans Ferry.

The bridge, or what was left of it, was left to deteriorate until around 1900, when the bridge franchise was purchased at a tax sale by the Perkins brothers, owners of the Horsehead Bridge Company. The brothers planned to take one of their other bridges, damaged by a severe flood, and reassemble it here. The bridge was a singletrack iron railroad bridge that had spanned the Susquehanna River at the town of Muncie.

Luckily for residents of the area who needed to cross the river, the Perkins brothers knew what they were doing. The first thing they did was to build new stone piers and raise them 6 feet above the height of the previous piers. Then they transported three pin-hung wrought-iron trusses to the site and assembled them on the newly constructed piers to create a bridge 530 feet long, 18 feet wide, with a vertical clearance of 11 feet and a weight limit of four tons.

The bridge was opened in November 1900 and has been open every day since— including Christmas, when you can go across for free—except for a week each summer when it's closed for inspection and maintenance. The two-lane bridge is constructed of wooden planks that rumble when you drive across—not because they are loose or unsafe but because of the way the planks are held in place. Besides, it's this rumble effect that gives the bridge its charm.

Tolls for automobiles are collected 24/7 (except for Christmas). Bicyclists cross for free as of this printing, but because the bridge is so narrow, it's closed to pedestrians. For more information visit www.dingmansbridge.com.

4 Ridgeline Trail

These stone fences were built by early farmers.

This hike is part of the Pocono Environmental Education Center. The trail is well marked and well maintained. You pass through the oak–chestnut forest and then descend from a steep ridge—with the help of a rope—to the gorge below, where you visit the ruins of a cabin and its abandoned earthen dam. Before you leave the forest, you come to a 15-foot waterfall on Alicia Creek (aka Spackmans Creek) and then hike alongside the stream back to your starting point.

Start: Pocono Environmental Education Center parking lot
County: Pike
Nearest town: Milford
Distance: 5.4-mile loop
Approximate hiking time: 2.5 to 3 hours
Difficulty rating: Moderate, due to a moderate climb
Terrain: Pine plantation, shale outcroppings, abandoned roads, forest footpath

Elevation gain: 100 feet
Land status: National recreation area
Other trail users: Environmental education students
Canine compatibility: Leashed dogs permitted
Fees/permits: No fees or permits required
Schedule: Education center building open year-round; trails open for hiking spring through fall, cross-country skiing and snowshoeing in winter

Trail contacts: Pocono Environmental Education Center, Dingmans Ferry; (570) 828-2319; www.peec.org
Delaware Water Gap National Recreation Area: Bushkill Falls; (570) 426-2435; www.nps.gov/dewa

Maps: USGS: Lake Maskenozha; Pocono Environmental Education Center maps and interpretive brochures

Finding the trailhead: From Hazleton drive north on Interstate 81 to Interstate 80 east. Continue east to exit 309 and take U.S. Route 209 north for 4 miles to the intersection of U.S. Business 209 and US 209. Turn right at the intersection to stay on US 209, and continue north for 14.3 miles. Turn left at the Pocono Environmental Education sign onto Briscoe Mountain Road, and continue 0.8 mile to the stop sign. Turn right onto Emery Road and drive to the Pocono Environmental Education Center parking lot. *DeLorme: Pennsylvania Atlas & Gazetteer:* Page 55 C4

The Hike

The Pocono Environmental Education Center (PEEC) wasn't always a learning center. Indeed, the center was built originally as a honeymoon resort, aptly named Honeymoon Haven. But all that changed when the federal government decided to build a dam on the Delaware River 6 miles upstream from the Delaware Water Gap at Tocks Island and started acquiring property along the river. In 1960 Pennsylvania, New York, New Jersey, Delaware, and the federal government formed the Delaware River Basin Commission to oversee the dam project, which was to begin in 1967 and be fully operational by 1975.

But the dam was not to be. One main problem was that the geology at the dam site was not capable of bearing the weight of the 160-foot-high dam. And of course there were many local residents and more than fifty environmental organizations opposed to the dam. After years of haggling and setbacks, the four states involved voted on whether to continue the project. When only Pennsylvania voted for the dam, the project was killed.

Today the PEEC is a learning center where students of all ages can come and observe Mother Nature's handiwork in one of the most delightful settings in the area. The Visitors Education and Administration Building houses classrooms, a library, a darkroom, an indoor pool, and a gift store. There are also forty-seven modern cabins and a dining hall.

Each trail at PEEC has a brochure that outlines and highlights what students and hikers will see along the trail.

The Ridgeline Trail is well worn and well blazed. At 1.5 miles you descend into the gorge using a rope to keep you from slipping. At 2.2 miles you come to a stone fireplace and chimney and the remains of a cabin that once sat on a bluff overlooking an earthen dam. If you're the least bit curious as you wander around the site and kick the

▶ *Pocono* **is a Native American word meaning "stream between two mountains."**

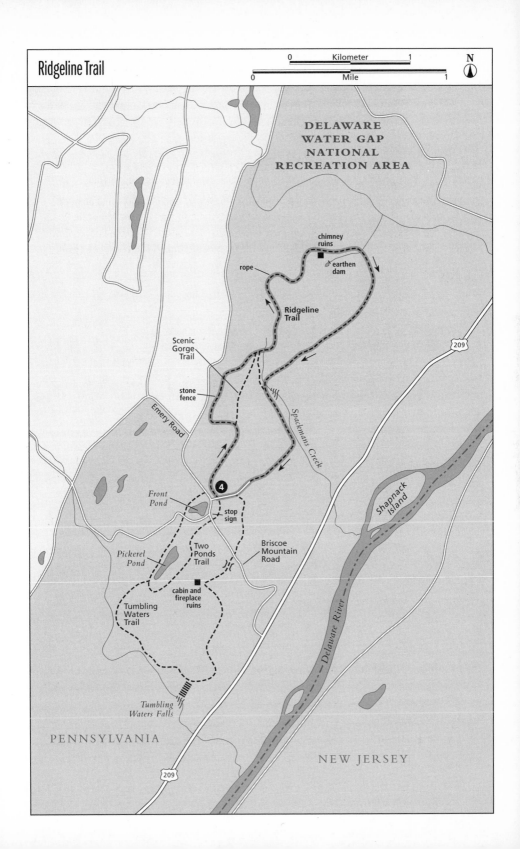

Ridgeline Trail

0   Kilometer   1

0   Mile   1

N

DELAWARE
WATER GAP
NATIONAL
RECREATION AREA

chimney
ruins

rope

earthen
dam

Ridgeline
Trail

209

Scenic
Gorge
Trail

stone
fence

Emery Road

Spackmans Creek

Shapnack
Island

4

Front
Pond

stop
sign

Pickerel
Pond

Two
Ponds
Trail

Briscoe
Mountain
Road

cabin and
fireplace
ruins

Tumbling
Waters
Trail

Delaware River

Tumbling
Waters Falls

PENNSYLVANIA

NEW JERSEY

209

foundation with your toe, you may wonder who built this cabin in such an idyllic spot and what happened to it? Did the cabin dwellers swim in the dammed water below and then race to the cabin to get warm by the fireplace?

At 3.0 miles you reach Alicia Creek and a 15-foot waterfall. Follow the creek for a while after the falls, and then return to the macadam road and civilization.

Miles and Directions

0.0 Start from the PEEC parking lot. Facing the building, the trail sign is to your left. The Ridge-line Trail is blazed yellow. The Scenic Gorge Trail is blazed red. Follow the yellow and the red blazes uphill.

0.2 Pass a small building on your left.

0.5 The red-blazed Scenic Gorge Trail turns right. Follow the yellow-blazed Ridgeline Trail to the left.

0.7 The trail passes through a stone boundary fence.

1.0 The Scenic Gorge Trail reconnects. Cross a stream. The Scenic Gorge Trail goes off to the right. Stay on the Ridgeline Trail.

1.7 The trail descends into the gorge. Use the rope to help you make your way down.

2.2 Pass a stone chimney and remains of a cabin, and descend to what was once an earthen dam.

3.0 Cross a stream above a 15-foot waterfall. Briefly connect with the red-blazed Scenic Gorge Trail and then turn left, following the yellow blazes.

5.0 Arrive at the cabin area and macadam road, and turn right onto the road.

5.4 Arrive back at the parking lot.

Hike Information

Local Information

Pocono Mountains Visitors Bureau: 1004 Main Street, Stroudsburg; (570) 421-5791 or (800) 762-6667; www.800poconos.com

Local Events/Attractions

Historic Dingmans Ferry Bridge: over the Delaware River, 1 mile east of the intersection of U.S. Route 209 and Route 739, www.dingmansbridge.com

Grey Towers National Historic Site: 151 Grey Towers Drive, Milford; (570) 296-9630; www.fs.fed .us/na/gt/; www.greytowers.org

Accommodations

The Dimmick Inn: 101 East Hartford Street, Milford; (570) 296-4021; www.dimmickinn

River Beach Campsites: 378 U.S. Routes 6/209, Milford; (570) 296-7421 or (800) 356-2852; www.kittatinny.com/pages/camping.php?page=camping

Restaurants

Apple Valley Restaurant: U.S. Route 6, Milford; (570) 296-6831; www.applevalleyrestaurant.com

Organizations
Pocono Outdoor Club: www.poconooutdoorclub.org

Local Outdoor Retailers
Pike County Outfitters: Apple Valley Village, U.S. Route 6, Milford; (570) 296-9492; www.pike countyoutfitters.net
Wal-Mart: U.S. Routes 6/209, Milford; (570) 491-4940

Hikers use a rope to help them down a steep cliff.

5 Tumbling Waters Trail

The upper falls at Tumbling Waters drop more than 60 feet into a deep pool.

This hike has everything. You start with a gentle stroll through a hardwood forest and pass through a pine plantation as the trail leads you to a picturesque lake. You then descend into a deep hemlock gorge to visit two torrential waterfalls. After the falls you visit the ruins of an old homestead and take in a panoramic view of the Delaware River Valley.

Start: Pocono Environmental Education Center parking lot
County: Pike
Nearest town: Milford
Distance: 3.3-mile loop
Approximate hiking time: 2 hours
Difficulty rating: Moderate except for short, strenuous climb out of a deep gorge
Terrain: Pine plantation, hemlock gorge, forest footpath, sandstone outcrop
Elevation gain: 390 feet
Land status: National recreation area

Other trail users: Environmental education students
Canine compatibility: Leashed dogs permitted
Fees/permits: No fees or permits required
Schedule: Education center building open year-round; trails open for hiking spring through fall, cross-country skiing and snowshoeing in winter
Trail contacts: Pocono Environmental Education Center, Dingmans Ferry; (570) 828-2319; www.peec.org
Delaware Water Gap National Recreation

Area, Bushkill Falls: (570) 426-2435; www.nps.gov/dewa
Maps: USGS: Lake Maskenozha; Pocono

Environmental Education Center trail maps and interpretive brochures

Finding the trailhead: From Scranton drive east on Interstate 84 and take exit 34. Turn right onto Route 739 and drive south for 13 miles to U.S. Route 209. Turn right onto US 209 and drive south for 4.8 miles. Turn right onto Briscoe Mountain Road and continue 0.8 mile to the stop sign. Turn right onto Emery Road and drive to the Pocono Environmental Education Center parking lot. *DeLorme: Pennsylvania Atlas & Gazetteer:* Page 55 C4

The Hike

What is it about waterfalls that fascinates us? Is it the sheer power of the water cutting its way through solid rock only to tumble willy-nilly from one ledge to the next? Is it the roar of the water that stops us in our tracks and turns a quiet forest into a place where you have to yell to be heard? Or do we identify with the water's unmatched tenacity as it continues its endless journey—day after day after day—as it has for thousands of years?

Whatever it is, if you like to get up close and personal to major waterfalls that get your heart racing with their beauty and power, this hike is for you.

Start at the Pocono Environmental Education Center (PEEC) parking lot and walk across Emery Road to the trail signs. In a clearing on your right, you'll pass a make-believe decomposition cemetery that depicts the evils of littering and the end result of our throwaway culture. One tombstone notes that Americans generate one waste tire per year per person for the entire U.S. population.

Before you get to Pickerel Pond, the trail passes through yet another stone boundary fence. The trail then cuts away from the pond and leads you through a pine plantation that was planted in the early part of the twentieth century. Stop and take a deep breath inside the plantation to learn just what those car fresheners shaped like pine trees are trying to smell like.

Highlights of this hike include the two waterfalls that cut their way through the bottom of a deep gorge. After you turn away from Pickerel Pond and make your way along the top of the gorge, you can hear the falls. As any experienced hiker will tell you, when you're approaching a major waterfall, you can hear it long before you can see it.

▶ **The Black Bear Film Festival is held each October in Milford.**

The descent into the gorge is made easier by switchbacks and wooden steps. It's fun going down: You hear the falls and for the moment forget that if you're going down, eventually you'll have to climb back up. The main falls take a roaring 60-foot drop into a deep pool. The second falls are farther downstream on Mill Creek, but you can view them only from above.

The ascent out of the gorge is rigorous, but once again there is a prize at the end of your struggle. As the trail levels off, it lands you on top of a ridge that provides an

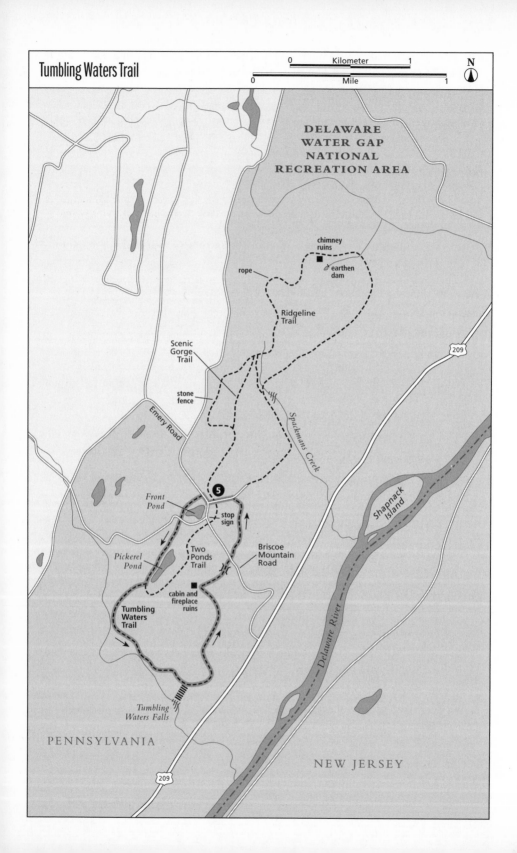

Tumbling Waters Trail

0 — Kilometer — 1

0 — Mile — 1

N

DELAWARE
WATER GAP
NATIONAL
RECREATION AREA

chimney
ruins
rope
earthen
dam

Ridgeline
Trail

Scenic
Gorge
Trail

stone
fence

209

Spackmans Creek

Emery Road

5

Front
Pond

stop
sign

Pickerel
Pond

Two
Ponds
Trail

Briscoe
Mountain
Road

Shapnack
Island

Tumbling
Waters
Trail

cabin and
fireplace
ruins

Delaware River

Tumbling
Waters Falls

PENNSYLVANIA

NEW JERSEY

209

exceptional view of the Delaware River Valley. From here the trail takes you past the ruins of an abandoned cabin. You then make your way back to cross Briscoe Mountain Road and turn onto Emery Road. If you look to your left as you walk uphill on Emery Road, you'll see a stone shrine, a giant ring, and an engraved headstone that explains the Legend of Aldyth. This was left over from when the PEEC was a honeymoon getaway.

Miles and Directions

0.0 Start from the PEEC parking lot. Cross Emery Road and walk toward the trail signs for the white-blazed Two Ponds Trail and orange-blazed Tumbling Waters Trail. Walk on the boardwalk for about 50 feet and pass a wildlife blind.

0.1 Pass an educational plaque about bats and a rock boundary fence on your left. Cross a feeder stream.

0.2 Cross Briscoe Mountain Road.

0.4 Arrive at Pickerel Pond near the dam. The trail turns right alongside the pond.

0.5 Turn right away from the pond.

0.7 The white-blazed Two Pond Trail goes off to your left. Stay on the Tumbling Waters Trail.

1.3 Turn right at the Tumbling Waters Trail sign.

1.4 Arrive at a wooden platform and steps leading down into the gorge.

1.6 Arrive at Tumbling Waters Falls. Retrace your steps back up the gorge and turn right at the trail.

2.0 Enjoy views of the Delaware River Valley.

2.2 Arrive at a stone fireplace and ruins of a small cabin.

2.5 Turn right at the Tumbling Waters Trail signpost.

2.8 Come to a bridge across a stream; turn left and then turn right, and cross Briscoe Mountain Road.

3.0 The trail turns right. The path to the log cabin goes off to your left. The blue-blazed Fossil Trail joins the Tumbling Waters Trail.

3.2 Turn left onto Emery Road.

3.3 Arrive back at the parking lot.

Hike Information

Local Information
Pocono Mountains Visitors Bureau: 1004 Main Street, Stroudsburg; (570) 421-5791 or (800) 762-6667; www.800poconos.com

Local Events/Attractions
Milford Music Festival: June, Milford; www.milfordmusic.org
Columns Museum: 608 Broad Street, Milford; (570) 296-8126; www.pikehistory.org

Accommodations

Dingmans Ferry Bed and Breakfast: 1087 Milford Road, Dingmans Ferry; (570) 828-1441; www .dingmansferrybedandbreakfast.com

Dingmans Campground: 1006 U.S. Route 209, Dingmans Ferry; (570) 828-1551 or (877) 828-1551; www.dingmanscampground.com

Restaurants

Muir House: 102 State Route 2001, Milford; (570) 296-6373; www.muirhouse.com

Organizations

Pocono Outdoor Club: www.poconooutdoorclub.org

Local Outdoor Retailers

Pike County Outfitters: Apple Valley Village, U.S. Route 6, Milford; (570) 296-9492; www.pikecounty outfitters.net/index.htm

Wal-Mart: U.S. Routes 6/209, Milford; (570) 491-4940

Shohola Falls.

6 Shohola Falls

The view from the observation tower shows the Shohola Waterfowl Management Area, a Pennsylvania Important Bird Area.

You first visit Shohola Falls as the tourists do. This hike then leads you to a rock ledge where you can view the falls from another vantage point. Then hike along Shohola Lake to an observation tower to view the Shohola Waterfowl Management Area, which has been classified as a Pennsylvania Important Bird Area.

Start: Shohola Falls Recreation Area parking lot on U.S. Route 6
County: Pike
Nearest town: Milford
Distance: 4.5 miles out and back
Approximate hiking time: 2.5 hours
Difficulty rating: Easy
Terrain: Forest footpaths, paved road, woods roads, streamside rock ledges
Elevation gain: 360 feet
Land status: State game lands

Other trail users: Hunters (in season), bird watchers, fishermen
Canine compatibility: Leashed dogs permitted
Fees/permits: No fees or permits required
Schedule: Year-round; caution advised during hunting seasons
Trail contacts: Pennsylvania Game Commission, Harrisburg; (717) 787-4250; www.pgc.state.pa.us
Maps: USGS: Pecks Pond, Edgemere, Shohola, Rowland

Finding the trailhead: From Scranton drive east on Interstate 84 and take exit 34. Turn left onto Route 739 and drive north for 0.7 mile. Turn right onto Weil Road and continue north for 3.8 miles. Turn right onto U.S. Route 6 and continue east for 2 miles to the Shohola Falls Recreation Area on your right. *DeLorme: Pennsylvania Atlas & Gazetteer:* Page 54 A4

The Hike

Shohola Falls is one of the most popular and most photographed waterfalls in the Poconos. On this hike you will see it first as tourists see it—from above near the dam and from a stone observation deck, both on the main parking lot side of the stream. But we also will view the falls from the west side of the stream, where there are two more stone observation decks and a set of rock steps that lead down to a narrow ledge at the edge of the plunge pool. This ledge is where you will get the best view of the falls and photographers will get their best shots.

After you walk to the dam, turn downstream, visit the observation deck, and then walk out to US 6. Cross the bridge and then continue on a forest footpath high above Shohola Creek to the dam on the other side of the stream. From this point you can walk down to the water level at the plunge pool for your best photos. But be careful here—the ledge can be wet and slippery.

You have made a U from one side of the dam to the other. When you return to the parking lot side, pick up a footpath near the restrooms that leads to the boat launch and then along the lake. You eventually get on a game lands road for a short stretch before returning to the lakeside to visit the observation tower, which affords an unobstructed view of Lake Shohola and the Shohola Waterfowl Management Area, the state game commission's wildlife propagation area on the west side of the lake.

The management area consists of the 1,100-acre lake, with two smaller islands and one larger island near the management area and 650 acres surrounding it at its southern end. Those 650 acres are made up of wetlands and northern bogs, and there are a number of dead standing trees, or "snags," which attract nesting birds. Because of all its natural attributes, the Shohola Waterfowl Management Area is classified as a Pennsylvania Important Bird Area.

▶ **The highest point in the Poconos is Mount Ararat in Wayne County. Elevation: 2,654 feet.**

Bald eagles were introduced here in the 1980s as part of the game commission's eagle restoration program, and they continue to do well here. Ospreys have also done well here, moving into empty eagles' nests when the eagles relocate to new ones.

If you're on the observation tower at the right time, you may observe wood ducks, common mergansers, American black ducks, mallards, and Canada geese. During migration and mating seasons, you could see loons, grebes, and diving and dabbling ducks.

The management area is closed to hunting and to the public. The lake itself is stocked with game fish, and fishing is allowed from shore and with electric-powered motorboats. Shohola Creek is a popular trout stream, even though the only way for

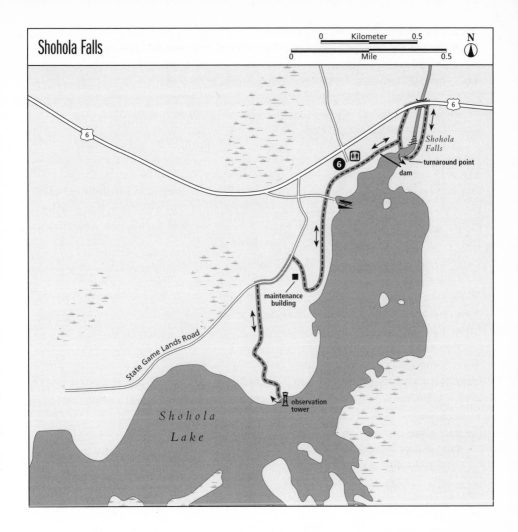

Shohola Falls

Shohola Lake

State Game Lands Road

maintenance
building

observation
tower

Shohola
Falls

turnaround point

dam

anglers to get to the stream is to walk. As you walk along this hike, you will see a number of "fisherman's paths" breaking off the main trail and descending down the steep ravine to the water's edge.

Shohola Creek changes little in elevation and more or less meanders its way into the lake. Because of its placid nature, local Native Americans named it *Shohola*, which in their language means "weak." But since the dam was built and the stream channeled into the sheer-walled chasm that creates the waterfalls, the waters of Shohola Creek are anything but placid.

Miles and Directions

0.0 Start at the parking lot and walk toward the trail sign and path. Continue into the forest to the restrooms, and turn left at the signs that read Dam and Overlooks.

0.1 Turn right onto the path that leads to the dam.

0.2 Arrive at the dam and Shohola Lake. Turn left onto the path that leads downstream to the overlook.

0.3 Continue downstream on the path alongside the railing.

0.5 Arrive at Old U.S. Route 6. Continue across the gulley toward US 6. (There is no clear path here.) Climb over the guardrails and turn right onto US 6. Walk across the US 6 bridge to the other side of Shohola Creek.

0.6 Arrive at the other side and turn right into the parking lot. Walk to the trail that enters the pine forest.

0.7 Veer left onto the trail that heads uphill.

0.9 Arrive at a paved parking lot. Turn right toward the falls and arrive at the upper observation deck. Continue down to the second overlook deck and turn right on the wooden steps.

1.0 Arrive at the rock surface. Turn left and walk along the edge. After viewing the falls retrace your steps back to the paved parking lot.

1.2 Arrive at the paved parking lot and turn left. Continue through the parking lot and pass a boat launch on your right. Come to a Y with two auto roads. Turn left and walk on the road back out to US 6.

1.4 Turn left onto US 6 and retrace your steps.

1.5 Turn left 25 feet before the end of the guardrails. Climb over the guardrails and cross the gulley on a path. Arrive at Old US 6 and turn right.

1.6 Arrive at the paved parking lot.

1.7 Turn left, heading toward the lake. Turn right onto the trail you began on and walk back through the picnic area to the restrooms. At the restroom area follow the sign that reads BOATING.

1.8 Turn left at a Y and head toward the lake.

2.0 Turn left at a T intersection and cross the paved boat-access road. Turn left onto a marshy path toward the lake.

2.3 Turn right onto the gravel road and walk past the maintenance building. Turn left onto the game lands road.

2.5 Turn left onto a grassy road. A sign here reads CLOSED TO ALL MOTOR VEHICLES.

2.7 A road comes in from your right. Continue to your left.

3.1 Arrive at the observation platform. Retrace your steps back toward the game lands road.

3.6 Keep right at the Y intersection.

3.7 Arrive back at the game lands road and turn right, retracing your steps back to the restroom area and the parking lot.

4.5 Arrive back at your vehicle.

Hike Information

Local Information

Pocono Mountains Visitors Bureau: 1004 Main Street, Stroudsburg; (570) 421-5791 or (800) 762-6667; www.800poconos.com

Local Events/Attractions

Autumn Arts & Craft Fair: September, Hawley; (570) 226-3191; www.lakeregioncc.com

Wayne County Historical Society Museum: 810 Main Street, Honesdale; (570) 253-3240; www .waynehistorypa.org

Accommodations

Laurel Villa Country Inn: Second and Ann Streets, Milford; (570) 296-9940; www.laurelvilla.com

Secluded Acres Campground: State Route 3040, Lakeville; (570) 226-9959

Restaurants

The Falls Port Inn & Restaurant: 330 Main Avenue, Hawley; (570) 226-2600; www.thefallsport innandrestaurant.com

Organizations

Pocono Outdoor Club: www.poconooutdoorclub.org

Local Outdoor Retailers

Pike County Outfitters: Apple Valley Village, U.S. Highway 6, Milford; (570) 296-9492; www.pike countyoutfitters.net

Wal-Mart: U.S. Routes 6/209, Milford; (570) 491-4940

GREY TOWERS

If you've got a few hours with nothing to do, I recommend a visit to Grey Towers National Historic Site in Milford. And don't worry about losing precious hiking time—after you park in the parking lot, which is at the bottom of the knoll, it's an uphill climb through mature trees and manicured lawn to get to the mansion.

The mansion itself, built by James Pinchot to resemble a medieval French chateau, was completed in 1886 as a summer home for his family. Much of the building materials were indigenous to the area. The slates for the roof came from New Jersey, the hemlock timbers were floated on rafts down the Delaware River from Lackawaxen, and the decorative bluestone used around the doors came from Shohola.

Pinchot's son Gifford inherited the house, and as Gifford became more active in Pennsylvania politics—he was governor twice—he used the mansion as his full-time residence until his death in 1946. Gifford's son Bryce donated the property to the USDA Forest Service in 1963. Call (570) 296-9639 or visit www.fs.fed.us/na/gt for more information.

7 Blooming Grove Trail

The Blooming Grove Trail passes through hemlock and pine forests.

This hike leads you over typical rocky footpaths and abandoned logging roads to a swampy area where you circumnavigate the Blue Heron Swamp. From there you come to the dark tannin-stained waters of Gates Run as you return to your starting point.

Start: Blooming Grove trailhead parking lot off Route 402
County: Pike County
Nearest town: Scranton
Distance: 5.0-mile lollipop
Approximate hiking time: 2.5 hours
Difficulty rating: Easy; mostly flat terrain with a few easy climbs
Terrain: Rocky, forest footpath; swampy sections; abandoned logging roads
Elevation gain: 300 feet

Land status: State forest
Other trail users: Hunters (in season)
Canine compatibility: Leashed dogs permitted
Fees/permits: No fees or permits required
Schedule: Year-round; caution advised during hunting seasons
Trail contacts: Delaware State Forest, Swiftwater; (570) 895-4000; www.dcnr.state.pa.us/FORESTRY/stateforests/delaware.aspx
Maps: USGS: Hawley

Finding the trailhead: From Scranton drive east on Interstate 84 and take exit 30. Turn left onto Route 402 and drive north for 3.9 miles. Turn left at the trail sign into the parking lot. *DeLorme: Pennsylvania Atlas & Gazetteer:* Page 54 A2

The Hike

Pennsylvania has more than 3,500 miles of hiking trails. Most of these trails have been built, and are maintained, by volunteers from regional hiking clubs, outdoor enthusiasts, conservation groups, and other regional service groups, such as the Boy Scouts and 4-H Clubs. Members of the Pike County 4-H Club built the Blooming Grove Trail in 1975 with assistance from employees of the Bureau of Forestry. Over time, maintenance on the trail faded, and by the late 1980s the trail was more or less unusable. In the early 1990s the Pocono Outdoor Club took over the trail maintenance, and today the trail is well groomed and well marked.

No doubt the 4-H leaders and members designed this hike so that they could get an up-close view of the Blue Heron Swamp and hopefully a great blue heron wading around in the swamp and poking its long, pointed bill into the water in search of it next meal, which could be a frog, a snake, a turtle, or even a small bird. The best time of day to spot a heron is either dusk or dawn; but they do spend their entire day searching for food. They walk slowly, stalking their prey; when they are ready to strike, they lunge quickly.

The best months to see great blue herons are March and April, when male and female herons take part in mating rituals. One sure way to distinguish this giant bird from other similar birds such as cranes is by its S-shaped neck. The heron—which stands

▶ **The lowest point in the Poconos is the village of Bushkill. Elevation: 340 feet.**

anywhere from 3 to 5 feet tall and has a wingspan of 6 feet—builds a large nest, sometimes 3 feet in diameter, very high in the tallest tree it can find.

While herons are not on the Endangered Species List, they are protected by the Migratory Bird Treaty Act. Herons are at risk, however, as each year more and more wetlands are lost to development.

The swamp and the swampy area surrounding it provide a diverse ecology for many forms of vegetation, trees, and wildlife. Depending on what season you hike this trail, you will see wild strawberries, raspberries, and blueberries and wildflowers such as violets and coneflowers. Check the swamp closely and you may see evidence of beavers hard at work. And check out the snags—dead trees that are still standing. Snags are the favored hangouts of woodpeckers, and every now and then you'll see a hawk perched on a limb scanning the swamp, waiting to swoop down and grab anything that moves.

The trail takes you to the edge of Gates Run, and for a short distance you walk along its bank. The waters of Gates Run are dark, looking as though someone had left a giant teabag soaking in the swamp. That is exactly what is happening: Acres of

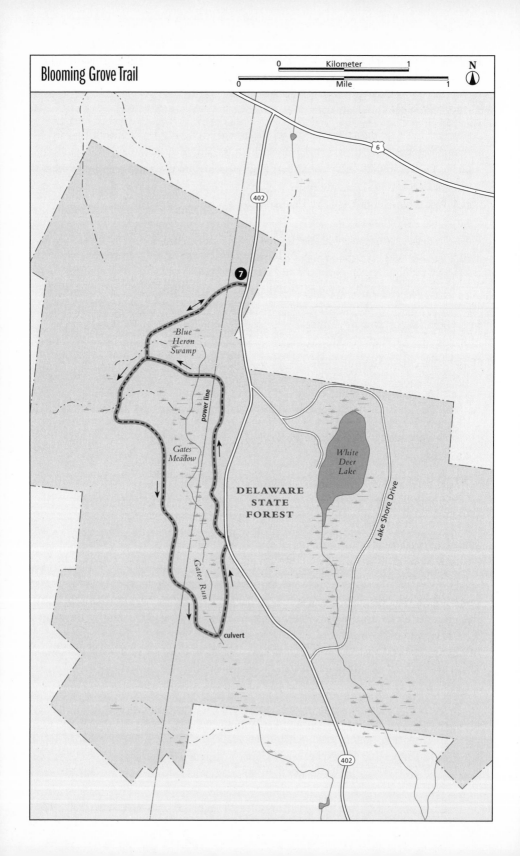

sphagnum moss absorb the tannin produced by the decaying plant life around the swamp and then, acting like a giant teabag, slowly release the tannin into the water.

Miles and Directions

0.0   Start at the parking lot. Walk toward the trail bulletin board and follow the trail arrow at the bulletin board. Cross the power-line swath and arrive at a trail map.

0.1   Enter the forest and follow the red-blazed Blue Heron Swamp Trail.

0.2   Bear right at the Y.

0.4   Pass the Blue Heron Swamp on your left.

0.6   Cross a small stream.

0.7   Turn right onto the white-blazed White Deer Trail at the trail register.

1.0   Turn right onto the blue-blazed Gates Meadow Loop.

1.1   Cross a small stream.

2.0   Pass through a marshy area and cross a stream.

2.2   Arrive at the power-line swath and turn right for about 50 feet to a blue arrow painted on a boulder. Turn left and walk toward the forest. Follow the blue blazes.

2.7   The trail turns left onto an abandoned road.

2.8   The trail turns left through an open area and you pass over the stream on a culvert.

3.4   Arrive beside Route 402 and then turn left into the forest.

3.7   Turn right at the blue blaze.

4.0   Turn left onto an abandoned road and jog right into the forest.

4.5   Turn left onto the white-blazed White Deer Trail.

4.6   Cross under the power line.

5.0   Arrive back at the trailhead and turn right to return to the parking lot.

Hike Information

Local Information
Pocono Mountains Visitors Bureau: 1004 Main Street, Stroudsburg; (570) 421-5791 or (800) 762-6667; www.800poconos.com

Local Events/Attractions
Steamtown National Historic Site: South Washington Avenue, Scranton; (570) 340-5200 or (888) 693-9391; www.nps.gov/stea

Electric City Trolley Station & Museum: Steamtown National Historic Site, South Washington Avenue, Scranton; (570) 963-6590; www.ectma.org/museum.html

Accommodations
The Settlers Inn: 4 Main Avenue, Hawley; (570) 226-2993; www.thesettlersinn.com

Wilsonville Camping Area: off U.S. Route 6, Hawley; (570) 226-4382

Restaurants
Gresham's Chop House: U.S. Route 6, Hawley; (507) 226-1500

Organizations
Pocono Outdoor Club: www.poconooutdoorclub.org

Local Outdoor Retailers
Dick's Sporting Goods: 600 Commerce Boulevard, Dickson City; (570) 963-1550
Wal-Mart: 900 Commerce Boulevard, Dickson City; (570) 383-2354
Wal-Mart: 777 Old Willow Avenue, Honesdale; (570) 251-9543

THE EAGLE INSTITUTE

Your best chance of seeing a bald eagle in the Poconos is on the Upper Delaware River during winter when Canadian lakes and rivers freeze over and these birds of prey migrate south to find open water. You may see a bald eagle floating downstream on an ice floe or perched on a tree branch along the shore, scanning the slate-gray water for the fish that will become its next meal.

If you've ever seen a bald eagle spread its wing and take flight, you know why the non-profit Eagle Institute has no problem getting volunteers to guide visitors to the best sites along the river. If you've never seen a bald eagle up close, what are you waiting for? You can spot bald eagles and other birds of prey during the other three seasons as well.

According to National Audubon Society estimates, in pre-colonial times there were 100,000 bald eagles in the lower forty-eight states. By the middle of the twentieth century, its records show that the bald eagle faced extinction in every state except Alaska. The culprit was the widely used pesticide DDT, which ended up in streams and rivers and, consequently, in the fish in these waterways. Bald eagles ingested the DDT along with the fish, which made their eggs so thin shelled that they broke before the embryos were ready to hatch.

The recovery of the bald eagle took decades, but today bald eagle nests have been reported in forty of Pennsylvania's sixty-seven counties. And it's agencies like the Eagle Institute—with its educational and tagging and tracking programs—that have kept the recovery, and the eagles, alive.

For more information visit the institute's Web site: www.eagleinstitute.org.

8 Shuman Point Natural Area

Lake Wallenpaupack lies right over the crest.

This is an easy, short hike through a state natural area and along the shoreline of Lake Wallenpaupack, one of the most popular recreational lakes in the Poconos. Along the way you will see a series of stone walls built when farmers cleared the site that was known, before the dam was built, as Wilsonville Village.

Start: Shuman Point Natural Area parking lot off Route 590
County: Wayne
Nearest town: Scranton
Length: 3.0-mile loop
Approximate hiking time: 1.5 hours
Difficulty rating: Easy
Terrain: Rocky, forest footpath; abandoned roads
Elevation gain: 240 feet
Land status: Private; owned by Pennsylvania Power & Light
Other trail users: Hunters (in season), anglers

Canine compatibility: Leashed dogs permitted
Fees/permits: No fees or permits required for hiking
Schedule: Year-round; caution advised during hunting seasons. The Wallenpaupack Environmental Learning Center is open weekdays and select weekends.
Trail contacts: Pennsylvania Power & Light Lake Office and the Wallenpaupack Environmental Learning Center, Hawley; (800) 354-8383; e-mail: pplpreserves@pplweb.com
Maps: USGS: Hawley

Finding the trailhead: From Scranton drive east on Interstate 84 and take exit 20. Turn left onto Route 507 and drive north for about 11 miles. Turn left onto U.S. Route 6 and continue around the head of Lake Wallenpaupack. Turn left onto Route 590 and continue for 2.1 miles. Turn left into the Shuman Point Natural Area parking lot. *DeLorme: Pennsylvania Atlas & Gazetteer:* Page 54 A2

The Hike

This hike takes you to the shores of 5,700-acre Lake Wallenpaupack. As anyone who has ever visited or read about the Pocono area knows, there are hundreds of lakes scattered across the Pocono Plateau. Most of these lakes were formed during the last ice age, when the glaciers that covered much of northeastern Pennsylvania retreated. The melting glaciers left behind the many large and small lakes and ponds that visitors see everywhere in the Poconos today.

Lake Wallenpaupack, however, is not a glaciated lake. It was built by the Pennsylvania Power & Light Company in 1926 to produce hydroelectricity. The lake is 13 miles long and 60 feet deep at its lowest point. PP&L still owns the lake, and part of the company's philosophy is to allow the lake to be used for boating and fishing and to allow parts of the surrounding shoreline to revert to natural areas. The 300-acre Shuman Point Natural Area is one of these areas.

The trail starts on an abandoned road that parallels most of the shoreline. Before the dam was built, the area surrounding Wallenpaupack Creek was a farming community known as Wilsonville Village. The original road was built to bring supplies to the farmers. There are old logging roads in the area as well, which give testimony that this stand of forest, like most of the forests in Pennsylvania, was logged until there were no more trees left to cut. The last logging took place here between 1910 and 1920.

As you hike the trail, you will note the second-growth forest is composed mostly of chestnut, white pine, red maple, and white oak. The trail also leads you through the ubiquitous stone fences that would-be farmers erected when they first tried farming the Pocono Plateau. The fences served two purposes: First they were places to stack the rocks that were taken from the field. Second, in some instances the stone fences served as property lines.

The trail has a few spurs leading to spots where you get a good view of the lake. In places where the trail is right at water level, you can see fishermen trails that will take you as close to the water as you want to get.

This is a short, easy hike. When you've completed it, you should have plenty of energy left to visit some of the other interesting sites on the lake. The Tafton Dike Observation Area is located at the intersection of US 6 and Route 507. The dike was built to prevent an overflow, but at the same time it created an excellent site from which to view Lake Wallenpaupack. You could rent a boat and try your luck at fishing. The lake is stocked with striped bass, and there are also small- and largemouth

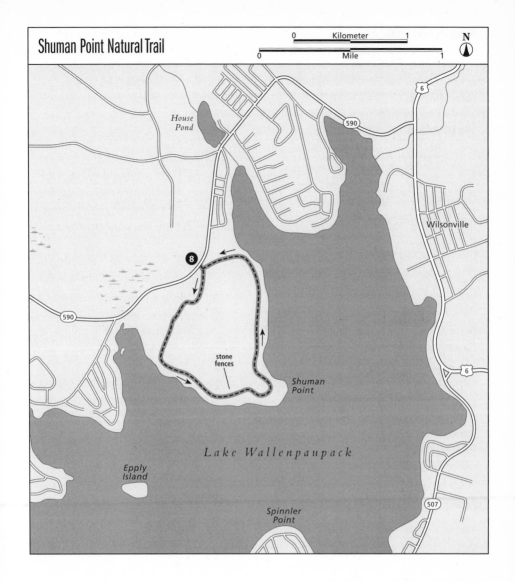

bass, rock bass, walleye, muskellunge, pickerel, rainbow trout, brown trout, and yellow perch.

If you run out of luck fishing, you could buy yourself a fish sandwich at one of the nearby restaurants, then get back in your boat and make your way to one of the lake's four islands to have a picnic.

If fishing is not your thing, PP&L puts on dozens of workshops and programs each month. For example, there are nineteen programs in the month of June, including "Backpacking in the 21st Century" and "Build Your Own Survival Kit."

Miles and Directions

0.0 Start at the parking lot. Walk to the trailhead bulletin board at the west side of the parking lot, and follow the blue blazes uphill.

0.3 The trail turns right and downhill.

0.8 Pass a trail on your right. Continue to follow the blue blazes.

1.1 Arrive at the edge of the lake.

1.7 Pass through stone boundary fences. The trail turns right, toward the lake.

2.4 Turn left onto an abandoned road.

3.0 Arrive at a gate and return to the parking lot.

Hike Information

Local Information

Pocono Mountains Visitors Bureau: 1004 Main Street, Stroudsburg; (570) 421-5791 or (800) 762-6667; www.800poconos.com

Local Events/Attractions

Wayne County Fair: August, Honesdale; (570) 253-5486; www.waynecountyfair.com

The Lacawac Sanctuary: Sanctuary Road, Lake Ariel; (570) 689-9494; www.lacawac.org

Accommodations

Beech Tree Gardens Bed and Breakfast: Route 590, Lake Ariel; (570) 226-8677

Caffrey Camping Area: 431 Lakeshore Drive, Lakeville; (570) 226-4608

Restaurants

The Boat House Restaurant: Route 507, Hawley; (570) 226-5027; www.the-boathouse-restaurant .com/cnt/cnt_hme.aspx

Organizations

Pocono Outdoor Club: www.poconooutdoor.org

Local Outdoor Retailers

Dick's Sporting Goods: 600 Commerce Boulevard, Dickson City; (570) 963-1550

Wal-Mart: 900 Commerce Boulevard, Dickson City; (570) 383-2354

Wal-Mart: 777 Old Willow Avenue, Honesdale; (570) 251-9543

9 Bruce Lake Natural Area

A hiker looks north at Egypt Meadow Lake.

This trail takes you through a rocky forest section as you hike toward the narrows of Egypt Meadow Lake, where you can view the dark waters of this man–made lake. The trail then follows an old logging road to spring-fed Bruce Lake, a glaciated lake. As you circle Bruce Lake, you'll come to an old-fashioned water pump.

Start: Bruce Lake Natural Area/Egypt Meadow parking lot off Route 390
County: Pike
Nearest town: Scranton
Distance: 7.4-mile lollipop
Approximate hiking time: 3.5 hours
Difficulty rating: Moderate
Terrain: Rocky, forest footpath; abandoned roads; marshy lakeside sections
Elevation gain: 320 feet
Land status: State forest
Other trail users: Hunters (in season), anglers

Canine compatibility: Leashed dogs permitted
Fees/permits: No fees or permits required
Schedule: Year-round; caution advised during hunting seasons
Trail contacts: Delaware State Forest, Swiftwater; (570) 895-4000; www.dcnr.state.pa.us/FORESTRY/stateforests/delaware.aspx
Promised Land State Park, Greentown; (570) 676-3428; www.dcnr.state.pa.us/stateparks/parks/promisedland.aspx
Maps: USGS: Promised Land; Promised Land State Park Trail System map

Finding the trailhead: From Scranton drive east on Interstate 84 and take exit 26. Turn right onto Route 390 and drive south for 0.1 mile. Turn left into the Bruce Lake Natural Area/Egypt Meadow parking lot. *DeLorme: Pennsylvania Atlas & Gazetteer:* Page 54 B2

The Hike

There are two provisos before starting this hike: First, there are two Bruce Lake Natural Area parking lots; be sure to start this hike at the northernmost parking area, which is just 0.1 mile south of I-84. This is also the parking area for Egypt Meadow. Second, if there are no trail maps at the trailhead bulletin board, contact the Promised Land State Park office and get a Promised Land Trail System map. The park office is just a few miles south of the trailhead off Route 390. Your best bet is to call the park office before you come to the area and ask them to mail you a map.

This map is the nicest and most comprehensive map that you are ever going to get from a state park or state forest. It shows all the trails—some 50 miles of trails for hiking, biking, horseback riding, cross-country skiing, and snowmobiling. The map covers the Bruce Lake Natural Area, the automobile roads within the state park and state forest, the various lakes and swamps, and nearby villages.

At a little over a mile into the hike, you get a good view of man-made Egypt Meadow Lake. The Civilian Conservation Corps built the sixty-acre lake in 1935 as part of President Franklin D. Roosevelt's plan to provide employment for young men during the Great Depression. And even though Roosevelt is remembered as having initiated the CCC on a national level, he based his model on Pennsylvania governor Gifford Pinchot's work camps that Pinchot had set up to build roads and other forest-related projects, such as the dam at Egypt Meadow.

Pinchot (1865–1946) graduated from Yale and went to France to study forestry. When he returned to the United States, he was recognized as the first American to be trained in forestry. He was named the first chief forester of the Division of Forestry, a position he held from 1898 to 1910.

Nationwide, more than 190,000 Pennsylvania residents served in the CCC, with 113 CCC camps from one end of the state to the other. In addition, Pennsylvania was chosen as the site of five of the National Park Service's Recreation Demonstration Areas. These areas were built to show that if recreation areas were built near enough to urban areas, urban dwellers would visit them. The plan worked, and in 1945 these areas—Blue Knob, Hickory Run, French Creek, Laurel Hill, and Raccoon Creek— were turned over to the Commonwealth, which in turn made them state parks.

After you cross the narrows of Egypt Meadow Lake, Bruce Lake Road leads to forty-eight-acre Bruce Lake, a glacial lake that is completely spring fed. For this reason its waters appear blue-green. Egypt Meadow Lake's waters are darker because tannin from nearby Balsam Swamp leaches into the lake. The trail circles the lake. Once you are back on Bruce Lake Road, retrace your steps back to the parking area.

Note: You can learn more about the Promised Land State Park trail-marking system in the Little Falls Trail hike.

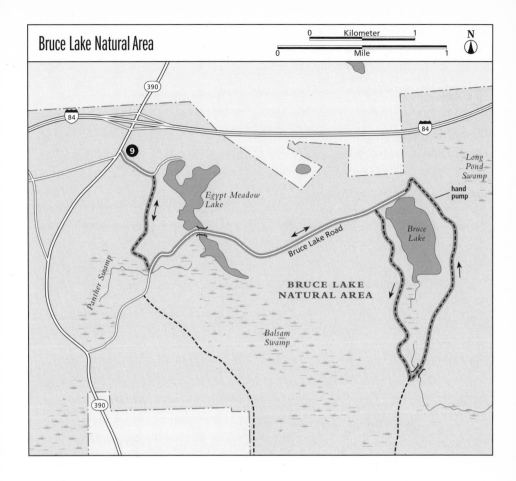

Miles and Directions

0.0 Start at the trailhead parking lot. Walk around the gate and get on the blue-blazed Egypt Meadows Road. (**Note:** All the trails are blazed blue.)

0.2 Turn right onto the Panther Swamp Trail.

0.3 Bear right to remain on the Panther Swamp Trail.

0.9 Turn left onto Bruce Lake Road.

1.3 Pass the Egypt Meadow Trail on your left.

1.5 Cross a bridge over the narrows of Egypt Meadow Lake.

2.5 Turn right onto the West Branch Trail.

3.7 Arrive at a bridge over Bruce Lake outlet. Turn left across the bridge.

4.3 Pass an old hand pump.

4.7 Arrive at a clearing at the head of the lake.

4.9 Pass the West Branch Trail on your left. You are now retracing your steps.

6.5 Turn right onto the Panther Swamp Trail.

7.2 Turn left onto Egypt Meadow Road.

7.4 Arrive back at the parking lot.

Hike Information

Local Information

Pocono Mountains Visitors Bureau: 1004 Main Street, Stroudsburg; (570) 421-5791 or (800) 762-6667; www.800poconos.com

Local Events/Attractions

Pike County Fair: August, Matamoras; (570) 296-8790

Mountain Creek Riding Stables: Route 940, Cresco; (570) 839-8725; www.mtcreekstable.com

Accommodations

Brookview Manor Inn: 2960 Route 447, Canadensis; (570) 595-2451; www.BrookviewManor.com

Martinville Streamside Cottages: Route 390, Canadensis; (570) 595-2489; www.martinville streamsidecottages.com

Promised Land State Park: camping and rustic cabins, Greentown; (570) 676-3428

Restaurants

The Homestead Inn: Sandspring Drive, Cresco; (570) 595-3171; www.thehomesteadinn.net

Organizations

Pocono Outdoor Club: www.poconooutdoorclub.org

Local Outdoor Retailers

Dick's Sporting Goods: 600 Commerce Boulevard, Dickson City; (570) 963-1550

Wal-Mart: 900 Commerce Boulevard, Dickson City; (570) 383-2354

Wal-Mart: 777 Old Willow Avenue, Honesdale; (570) 251-9543

Wal-Mart: 500 Route 940, Mount Pocono; (570) 895-4700

DANIEL BEARD

Although Daniel Beard (1850–1941) was born in Ohio, he is remembered by many Pocono historians as one of the most illustrious—and famous—characters to hit the shores of Lake Teedyuskung. In his head-to-toes buckskins, campaign hat, and white-bearded face, Beard was hard to miss.

Beard, who started out as a civil engineer and then became an illustrator, magazine editor, and author, gained international fame in 1889 when he illustrated Mark Twain's *A Connecticut Yankee in King Arthur's Court.*

But perhaps Beard is best known as one of the founders of the Boy Scouts of America in 1910. Prior to 1910 he had started "The Sons of Daniel Boone, a Boy's Outdoor Club," which he merged with Ernest Seton's "Woodcraft Indians" to form the Boy Scouts of America. Using his skills as an illustrator, he designed the original Scout uniform—the hat, shirt, and neckerchief.

Beard was named the first National Scout Commissioner, and he remained active in the Boy Scouts in one way or another until his death.

Beard owned three parcels of land on Lake Teedyuskung in Pike County, which he called Wild Lands. His brother Frank owned land next to Beard's, and it was on Frank's land that the brothers started the first Boy Scout camp in the United States.

In 1882 Beard wrote and illustrated *What to Do and How to Do It: The American Boy's Handy Book.* Throughout his life he continued to write and illustrate outdoor activity books for boys and girls. He wrote a total of twenty-one books—eight of which are still in print. His monthly column in the Boy Scout magazine, *Boys Life,* became one of the magazine's most popular and enduring features.

Even today, Beard's love of the outdoors is a viable part of many youngsters' lives. His most popular book, *The American Boy's Handy Book,* has sold more than 250,000 copies and continues to sell today.

10 Little Falls Trail

A footbridge crosses East Wallenpaupack Creek.

This easy hike would make a great family hike. Essentially the trail runs alongside the east branch of Wallenpaupack Creek, crosses it on a wooden footbridge, continues to the park boundary, and then returns along the other side of the stream to the trail's starting point. As with all waterfalls, it's best to view the falls in early spring or fall or after a rainy period.

Start: Lower Lake Dam parking area, Promised Land State Park
County: Pike
Nearest town: Scranton
Distance: 2.9 miles out and back with loop
Approximate hiking time: 1.5 hours
Difficulty rating: Easy
Terrain: Grass footpath, forest footpath, abandoned roads, creekside boulders
Elevation gain: 50 feet
Land status: State park

Other trail users: Hunters (in season), anglers
Canine compatibility: Leashed dogs permitted
Fees/permits: No fees or permits required
Schedule: Year-round; caution advised during hunting seasons
Trail contacts: Promised Land State Park, Greentown; (570) 676-3428; www.dcnr.state .pa.us/stateparks/parks/promisedland.aspx
Maps: USGS: Promised Land; Promised Land State Park Trail System map

Finding the trailhead: From Scranton drive east on Interstate 84 and take exit 26. Turn right onto Route 390 and drive south for approximately 4 miles. Turn right onto Lower Lake Road and enter the park. Continue on Lower Lake Road for 1.8 miles to the parking lot on your right, just past the dam. *DeLorme: Pennsylvania Atlas & Gazetteer:* Page 54 B2

The Hike

This hike is part of the extensive Promised Land Trail System, which is contained within Promised Land State Park and the surrounding Delaware State Forest. This system is unique: All its trails are blazed in blue, and the trail markers are numbered and have directional arrows pointing the way from one marker to the next. As with all well-marked trails, when you are approaching a trail intersection, there is a double blaze, which indicates an upcoming intersection or that the trail turns to the right or left.

Although you don't need the park map to do this hike, I suggest stopping at the park office to pick up a copy of the trail system map so that you can get an over-view of all the sites and activities in the park. You can also check out the trail marker numbering system and see how it applies to this hike. The park hike is a mere 1.0 mile long. Our hike extends that hike along the stream to include a trek through the hardwood and hemlock forest to the park boundary and back to the stream, where you will return along the opposite side.

This hike is great for children, outdoor photographers, and nature lovers who just want to take a walk in a beautiful spot where the only sound is the rushing of clear mountain water. The trail leads alongside the east branch of Wallenpaupack Creek, the stream that was dammed back in 1926 by the Pennsylvania Power & Light Company to create Wallenpaupack Lake and produce hydroelectricity. The PP&L still owns the lake and still produces electricity. Today Wallenpaupack Lake is a major attraction for tourists, boaters, and fishermen.

Wallenpaupack Creek is a torrential stream that sends water cascading over the flattened boulders that create one waterfall after another after another. There are plenty of photo ops at the 0.5-mile point near the footbridge. There are just as many—or more—photo ops when you return on the other side of the creek.

▶ Rudolph von Hoevenberg opened the first honeymoon resort in the Poconos, The Farm on the Hill, in 1945.

Like most of Pennsylvania's forests, the forest that once existed where the park is now located was repeatedly clear-cut until, by the early 1900s, there were no trees left and most of the wildlife had migrated from the area. It was at that low point in 1902 that the Commonwealth bought the land and worked to reclaim the area and the forest. After a few years the wildlife returned, and in 1905 the state opened Promised Land State Park, its fourth state park.

During the Great Depression of the 1930s, young men from the Civilian Conservation Corps were brought to the area and given a number of forest projects to work

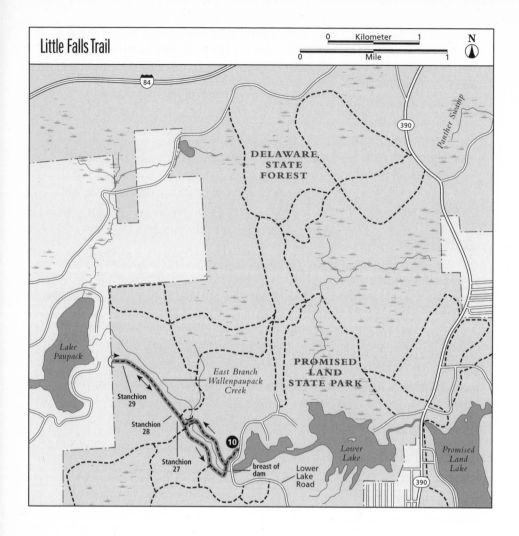

on. If you are curious as to what life was like back then for these young men, you can rent one of the twelve cabins they built. The cabins are unchanged since that time except for a few modern conveniences, such as electricity and nearby showers.

No matter where you choose to spend the night, the Little Falls Trail is a definite must-do hike. To make it even better, be sure to bring your children and/or your significant other, your camera, and your lunch. It's that kind of a place.

Miles and Directions

0.0 Start at the parking lot on Lower Lake Road just past Lower Lake Dam. Cross the road and walk toward the breast of the dam. Turn right before you reach the dam, and follow the blue blazes.

0.5   Arrive at the bridge across the stream. Turn left and cross the stream. Turn right on the other side of the bridge; walk about 50 feet and turn left, heading toward Stanchion 27.

0.6   Arrive at Stanchion 27 and turn right onto an abandoned road, heading toward Stanchion 28.

0.7   Arrive at Stanchion 28 and head toward Stanchion 29.

0.8   Cross a small stream.

1.3   Enter a pine forest.

1.4   Arrive at Stanchion 29. Retrace your steps toward the bridge.

2.4   Arrive at the bridge, but do not cross it. Turn right just before the bridge, and follow the blue blazes across the boulders.

2.8   Turn left onto the wooden bridge below the dam, and retrace your steps across the road.

2.9   Arrive back at the parking lot.

Hike Information

Local Information
Pocono Mountains Visitors Bureau: 1004 Main Street, Stroudsburg; (570) 421-5791 or (800) 762-6667; www.800poconos.com

Local Events/Attractions
Greene-Dreher-Sterling Agricultural Fair: August–September, Newfoundland; (570) 676-4047; www.gdsfair.com
Dorflinger Glass Museum/Dorflinger-Suydam Wildlife Sanctuary; Wildflower Music Festival: summer, Long Ridge Road, White Mills; (570) 253-1185; www.dorflinger.org

Accommodations
The Merry Inn Bed and Breakfast: Route 390, Canadensis; (570) 595-2011 or (800) 858-4182; www.themerryinn.com
Promised Land State Park: camping and rustic cabins, Greentown; (570) 676-3428

Restaurants
Ehrhardt's Waterfront Restaurant: 205 Route 507, Hawley; (570) 226-2124; www.Ehrhardts.com

Organizations
Pocono Outdoor Club: www.poconooutdoorclub.org

Local Outdoor Retailers
Dick's Sporting Goods: 600 Commerce Boulevard, Dickson City; (570) 963-1550
Gander Mountain: 955 Viewmont Drive, Dickson City; (570) 347-9077; www.gandermountain.com
Wal-Mart: 777 Old Willow Avenue, Honesdale; (570) 251-9543

11 Pennel Run

The bridge across Spruce Run was built by volunteers to withstand flooding.

This hike is rated moderate, mostly due to a moderate elevation gain and a rocky section for the first mile or so. The trail runs alongside Spruce Run—a pristine mountain stream—then passes through a state natural area. This hike is well worth taking, if only to see the unique bridge that volunteers from the Keystone Trails Association built over Spruce Run.

Start: Pennel Run trailhead on Snow Hill Road
County: Pike
Nearest town: East Stroudsburg
Length: 7.0-mile lollipop
Approximate hiking time: 4 hours
Difficulty rating: Moderate
Terrain: Very rocky footpath; grassy abandoned road
Elevation gain: 700 feet
Land status: State forest

Other trail users: Hunters (in season), backpackers, campers
Canine compatibility: Leashed dogs permitted
Fees/permits: No fees or permits required
Schedule: Year-round; caution advised during hunting seasons
Trail contacts: Delaware State Forest, Swiftwater; (570) 895-4000; www.dcnr.state.pa.us/FORESTRY/stateforests/delaware.aspx
Maps: USGS: Twelve Mile Pond, Skytop; Delaware State Forest; Thunder Swamp Trail System

Finding the trailhead: From New Jersey cross the Delaware River on the Interstate 80 bridge and take exit 309. Turn right onto U.S. Route 209 and drive north 4 miles to the intersection with Business U.S. 209 and Route 402. Turn left onto Route 402 and drive for 10.2 miles. Turn left onto Snow Hill Road and continue for 2.3 miles to the parking lot on your right. *DeLorme: Pennsylvania Atlas & Gazetteer:* Page 54 C3

The Hike

The Youth Conservation Corps built the Thunder Swamp Trail System in the 1970s. It comprises 43 miles of interconnecting trails that lie in the southern region of the Delaware State Forest—80,267 acres in Pike, Monroe, Northampton, and Carbon Counties. The main trailhead for the system is located on Route 402 in Marshalls Creek, 8.4 miles north of the intersection of Route 402 and US 209 or 1.8 miles south of Snow Hill Road. This main trailhead information is for reference only; we will not be going there on this hike.

As any experienced hiker knows, there are plenty of rocky hiking trails in Pennsylvania. In fact, some Appalachian Trail thru-hikers say that the stretch of the AT that passes through Pennsylvania is home to some of the rockiest hiking on the entire trail. And so it is in the Poconos: There are plenty of rocks, affectionately called "Pocono potatoes," scattered liberally on many hikes.

The very beginning of the Pennel Run Trail, say the first mile or so, is not just rocky. Many of the rocks are pointed upward, like arrowheads, and while we all know not to step on that point, there are times when you stumble or lose your footing and end up stepping down on one of these points. Ouch! This is one trail where you definitely need sturdy hiking boots.

At a little over 0.5 mile, you reach Spruce Run; in another 0.3 mile you cross the stream on a wooden footbridge set on three huge wire baskets full of—what else—rocks. The bridge was built by volunteers from the Keystone Trails Association. It's an interesting construction, and surely, with that much foundation, it would take a flood of biblical proportions to wash it away. The bridge is also interesting because it is a two-lane affair: Instead of having handrails on each side, it has one lone handrail in the middle.

From the bridge the trail turns left at the intersection with the connector trail. After a short climb over a ledge, you reach a plateau of sorts and Hay Road. Turn left onto Hay Road and walk a little over 0.5 mile, where you need to watch for the double red blazes that signify a right turn into the forest and the natural area.

Natural areas, as the name implies, are meant to be left in their natural state. The trail through here is blazed but otherwise is affected only by hikers repeatedly walking the same trail. Take your time here, and be sure you see the blazes before you continue forward.

After 2 miles of hiking through the natural area, climb back out of the ravine and reconnect with Hay Road. From there retrace your steps back to the beginning.

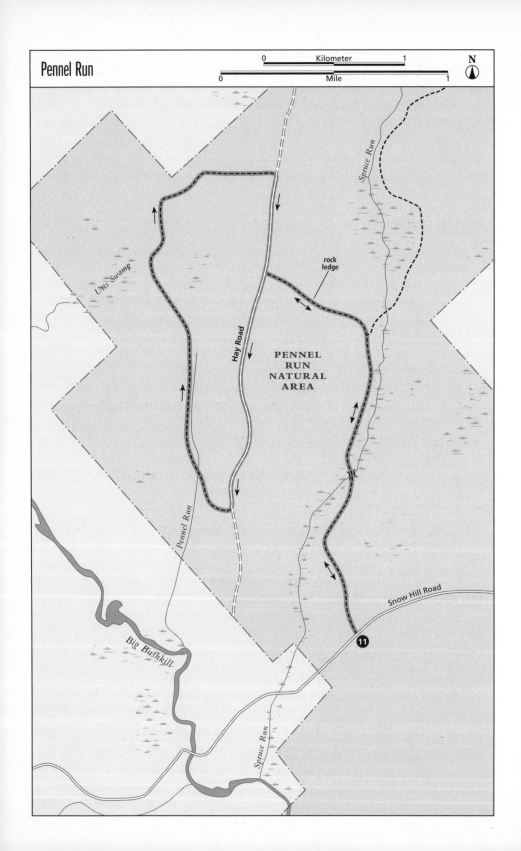

Pennel Run

When you are on this hike—and indeed on many of the hikes in Delaware State Forest—you may feel like you and your hiking companions are all alone in the woods. And you may be. But be aware that many of the trails here are multiuse. Many are open to horseback riders, mountain bikers, and ATV riders, as well as snowmobilers in winter. In addition, the forest is open to hunting in season. If you're hiking in late fall or winter, it's always smart to check the Pennsylvania Game Commission Web site (www.pgc.state.pa.us; type "hunting season" in the subject search field) to see if there is a hunting season in effect. And always wear orange and carry a whistle to let hunters know you're out there.

Miles and Directions

Note: The path that leads north out of the parking lot and into the woods is not part of our hike.

0.0 Start at your vehicle and walk back to Snow Hill Road. Turn right onto Snow Hill Road and walk about 20 feet to the trailhead on your right. Follow the orange blazes to the trail register.

0.6 Arrive at Spruce Run. The trail turns right.

0.8 Cross a feeder stream that empties into Spruce Run.

0.9 Cross Spruce Run on a wooden footbridge.

1.0 The trail turns left at double orange blazes.

1.5 Come to a trail intersection and turn left onto the red-blazed trail. The trail sign reads PENNEL RUN NATURAL 0.5 MILE. The orange-blazed trail continues straight.

1.8 Begin a steep climb up a ledge.

2.0 Turn left onto Hay Road.

2.7 Turn right at the double red blazes off Hay Road and onto a footpath into the woods.

2.9 Cross Pennel Run on mossy rocks and turn right.

4.8 Arrive back at Hay Road; turn right.

5.0 Arrive at the intersection (where you began the loop) with the red-blazed connector trail. Turn left and retrace your steps back to the trailhead.

7.0 Arrive back at your vehicle.

Hike Information

Local Information

Pocono Mountains Visitors Bureau: 1004 Main Street, Stroudsburg; (570) 421-5791 or (800) 762-6667; www.800poconos.com

Local Events/Attractions

Shawnee Mountain Ski Area, Shawnee-on-Delaware: Rodeo & Chili Cook-off (September) and Autumn Timber & Balloon Festival (October); (570) 421-7231; www.shawneemt.com

Pocono Snake and Animal Farm: Seven Bridge Road (Route 209), Marshalls Creek; (570) 223-8653; www.poconosnakeandanimalfarm.com

Accommodations

The Gatehouse Country Inn: River Road, Shawnee-on-Delaware; (570) 420-4553; www.gate
housecountryinn.com
Delaware Water Gap KOA: 233 Hollow Road, East Stroudsburg; (570) 223-8000; www.delaware
watergapkoa.com

Restaurants

Brandli's Pizza Pasta Vino: 300 Foxmoor Village, U.S. Route 209, Marshall's Creek; (570) 223-1600

Organizations

Pocono Outdoor Club: www.poconooutdoorclub.org

Local Outdoor Retailers

Dunkleberger's Sports Outfitters: 585 Main Street, Stroudsburg; (570) 421-7950
Wal-Mart: 355 Lincoln Avenue, East Stroudsburg; (570) 424-8415

POCONO FIRSTS

The first railroad built in the United States was built between Jim Thorpe and Summit Hill, Carbon County, in 1827.

In 1829 the first steam locomotive in the United States, the Stourbridge Lion, made its trial run on the Gravity Railroad in Honesdale, Wayne County.

The first commercial ski resort in the state started in 1946 at Big Boulder Ski Area; in 1956 the resort introduced man-made snow.

The first silent movie made in the United States was filmed in Milford, Pike County, in 1912.

The first Boy Scout camp in the United States was established circa 1910 at Lake Teedyuskung, Milford, Pike County.

Inspired by Pocono winters, Honesdale resident Dick Smith wrote the song "Winter Wonderland."

Gifford Pinchot of Milford was the first chief of the United States Department of Agriculture Forest Service.

12 Mount Minsi

Many Appalachian Trail thru-hikers consider this section of the AT one of the rockiest stretches of the entire trail.

Try this hike, which is part of the Appalachian Trail, for a steady uphill climb over rocks and boulders. Along the way to the top, you get spectacular views of the Delaware River and the steady stream of traffic on the Interstate 80 bridge. Once on top, you reach a flat area where you can view the ruins of a fire tower and then check out the once-in-a-lifetime view of the Delaware River as it winds its way into New Jersey.

Start: From the parking lot for Lake Lenape
County: Monroe
Nearest town: Stroudsburg
Distance: 4.9 miles out and back
Approximate hiking time: 3 hours
Difficulty rating: Moderate; plenty of climbing over boulders and a rocky trail
Terrain: Mountain footpath over rocks and through outcroppings; a climb along the rocky edge of a water gap

Elevation gain: 1,221 feet
Land status: National recreation area
Other trail users: Backpackers
Canine compatibility: Leashed dogs permitted
Fees/permits: No fees or permits required
Schedule: Year-round
Trail contacts: Delaware Water Gap National Recreation Area, Bushkill Falls; (570) 426-2435; www.nps.gov/dewa
Maps: USGS: Stroudsburg

Finding the trailhead: From Scranton drive south on Interstate 380 and connect with Interstate 80, heading east toward Stroudsburg. Take exit 310 and drive south on Route 611 for 0.6 mile to the stoplight in the town of Delaware Water Gap. Turn left at the stoplight onto Route 611 south and drive 0.3 mile. Turn right onto Mountain Road and drive 0.1 mile. Turn left at the fork, and drive to the Lake Lenape parking lot. *DeLorme: Pennsylvania Atlas & Gazetteer:* Page 68 A2

The Hike

The town of Delaware Water Gap has the air of an alpine skiing village. The town is small and its outskirts look like any other small Pennsylvania town, but as soon as you reach the downtown area, you get the feeling something outdoorsy is happening around the place.

Something is happening: The Appalachian Trail passes through town. You get the feeling that residents are used to seeing weary hikers plodding into their town for a little R&R. One cafe on the main street sums up the feeling with its name, the Trails End Cafe.

The town of Delaware Water Gap is also the southern terminus of the Delaware Water Gap National Recreation Area—a 70,000-acre recreation paradise that runs for 40 miles on both the Pennsylvania and the New Jersey sides of the Delaware River and hosts more than eight million visitors a year.

At the center of all this activity is the Delaware River. Even though it's just the twenty-fifth largest river in the country, its importance cannot be overstated. Despite its relative size, the Delaware provides 10 percent of the nation's population with water. Even more remarkable, its water is clean and it is one of the few remaining free-flowing rivers in the country. To recognize this small miracle, this section of the Delaware has been designated a Middle Delaware Scenic and Recreation River and a National Scenic River.

One of the popular activities here is river camping, which involves canoeing a stretch of the river and stopping for the night at one of the many riverside campsites along the way. Within the park boundaries the river is a series of shallow riffles and quiet pools, with no difficult rapids. There are access points every 8 to 10 miles, which allow for easy day trips. Or boaters can camp (for one night only) in one of the primitive campsites along the river. Tubing and rafting are allowed as well. A number of local liveries rent tubes, rafts, and canoes and offer both launch and pickup services.

Whether it's a leisurely sightseeing tour along the Delaware or a more aggressive ride on a mountain bike, there are a number of bicycle trails inside and outside the park. The longest touring route is the Old Mine Road, which is on the New Jersey side and runs the length of the park. Mountain bike riders can check out the Zion Church Road for a ride past Hidden Lake and the historic Zion Church and cemetery.

There are more than 20 ice-climbing and 200 rock-climbing sites in the park, with levels ranging from novice to advanced. Climbers don't have to register with the park, but park officials recommend that climbers tell a friend where they intend to climb and give them the park's twenty-four-hour emergency number (800-543-4295).

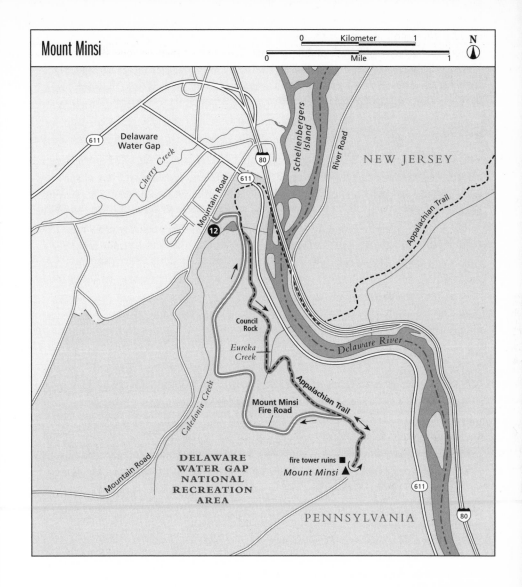

Mount Minsi

Delaware Water Gap

Cherry Creek

Mountain Road

Schellenbergers Island

River Road

NEW JERSEY

Appalachian Trail

Council Rock

Eureka Creek

Caledonia Creek

Delaware River

Mount Minsi Fire Road

Appalachian Trail

Mountain Road

DELAWARE WATER GAP NATIONAL RECREATION AREA

fire tower ruins ■
Mount Minsi ▲

PENNSYLVANIA

0   Kilometer   1
0   Mile   1

N

This hike starts at the trailhead for the Appalachian Trail, just a few blocks south of town at the parking lot of tiny Lake Lenape. Because this is a popular spot for tourists and locals, when you start out you get the feeling that the trail will be crowded. But as soon as you begin the first serious climb, you realize that your fellow hikers have opted to stay low. It's just you and the boulders, proving once again what all serious hikers have always known: When the air gets thin, so does the crowd.

Just 0.5 mile into the hike you get your first vista. Standing on an outcrop, you can see the cars and 18-wheelers whizzing along I-80. Interestingly, while you can see the traffic, you won't hear it. Not only are there no crowds this high up, but there is no traffic noise either. As you climb higher and higher up the rocky cliff edge of Mount Minsi, the trucks and cars get smaller and smaller each time you stop for a view until, when you reach the summit, the vehicles are indistinguishable from the roadway.

After hugging the cliff edge for a mile, you come to a sign that reads VIEW TRAIL. This is a little confusing, but what it means is there is a view 15 feet or so straight ahead. After you walk out to it, return to the sign and continue uphill. From this point the trail cuts away from the rim and into the forest for your last, short climb to the summit of Mount Minsi—a flat, open area where a fire tower once stood. All that remains of the tower is a set of stone steps and the concrete pylons where the tower legs were anchored into the earth. When you feel the force of the wind as it whips up out of the gap, you get an idea of what it must have been like in that tower. But like all the other fire towers in the state, this one was shut down when the Forest Service began using small airplanes to monitor forest fires.

▶ In 1725 Nicholas Depui established the first permanent residence in the Poconos—Shawnee in Monroe County.

It's lonely at the top. There's not much else up here but the wind and a fenced-in microwave tower hanging on the edge of the cliff. There's a grove of table mountain pine trees, and in one of them there's a sign that says MOUNT MINSI.

Miles and Directions

0.0 Start at the Lake Lenape parking lot. Walk to the iron access gate across the Mount Minsi Fire Road and the trailhead bulletin board. Turn left onto a paved path and follow the white blazes of the Appalachian Trail.

0.1 Cross the breast of Lake Lenape. Start an uphill climb.

0.3 Turn left at the double white blazes. Note that the blazes are on a tree on your right. Stay to the left at the fork in the trail.

0.4 Arrive at the first outcropping for a view of I-80.

0.5 Come to an outcropping with a sign that reads COUNCIL ROCK.

1.1 Cross a stream with a Eureka Creek sign.

1.2 Turn right at the View Trail sign.

1.9 Reach a flat area. Turn left onto the Mount Minsi Fire Road; walk 50 feet and then turn right onto the white-blazed Appalachian Trail.

2.2 Reach the summit of Mount Minsi. Retrace your steps back to the Mount Minsi Fire Road.

2.5 Turn right onto the Mount Minsi Fire Road, and begin your descent.

2.6 Pass the Appalachian Trail on your left, then again on your right. Continue straight on the fire road.

4.6 Pass the Appalachian Trail on your right.

4.8 Arrive at Lake Lenape.

4.9 Arrive back at the parking lot.

Hike Information

Local Information

Pocono Mountains Visitors Bureau: 1004 Main Street, Stroudsburg; (570) 421-5791 or (800) 762-6667; www.800poconos.com

Twenty-four-hour fall foliage/ski hotline (in season): (570) 421-5565

Tourist information and free brochures: (570) 424-6050 or (800) 762-6667

Local Events/Attractions

Water Gap Trolley: Tour points of interest on an antique-style trolley. 1 Main Street, Delaware Water Gap; (570) 476-9766; www.watergaptrolley.com

Quiet Valley Living Historical Farm: 1000 Turkey Hill Road, Stroudsburg; (570) 992-6161; www.quietvalley.org

Accommodations

The Shepard House Bed and Breakfast: Shepard Avenue, Stroudsburg; (570) 424-9779; www.shepardhouse.com/welcome.html

Mountain Vista Campground: 50 Taylor Drive, Stroudsburg; (570) 223-0111; www.mtnvistacampground.com

Restaurants

Sycamore Grill: Main and Oak Streets, Delaware Water Gap; (570) 426-1200; www.sycamoregrille.com

Organizations

Pocono Outdoor Club: www.poconooutdoorclub.org

Local Outdoor Retailers

Dunkleberger's Sports Outfitters: 585 Main Street, Stroudsburg; (570) 421-7950

Wal-Mart: 355 Lincoln Avenue, East Stroudsburg; (570) 424-8415

13 Wolf Swamp and Deep Lake

Wolf Swamp may be the most picturesque swamp many hikers have ever seen.

Sometimes you come across a hike that is different simply because of its features. This is one of those hikes. First you come to a unique and picture-perfect swamp that looks more like a mountain lake than a swamp. Then you reach a perfectly round glacial lake that will inspire you with its beauty and serenity. Bring your camera.

Start: State Game Lands 38 parking lot on Camelback Road
County: Monroe
Nearest town: East Stroudsburg
Distance: 4.3-mile loop
Approximate hiking time: 2.5 hours
Difficulty rating: Easy, with a final 1.2-mile steep ascent
Terrain: Rocky woods roads, grassy footpaths, abandoned railroad grade, power line right-of-way
Elevation gain: 540 feet
Land status: State game lands
Other trail users: Hunters (in season),
mountain bikers
Canine compatibility: Leashed dogs permitted
Fees/permits: No fees or permits required
Schedule: Year-round; caution advised during hunting seasons
Trail contacts: Pennsylvania Game Commission, Harrisburg; (717) 787-4250; www.pgc.state.pa.us
   Big Pocono State Park, Tannersville, c/o Tobyhanna State Park, Tobyhanna; (570) 894-8336; www.dcnr.state.pa.us/stateParks/parks/bigpocono.aspx
Maps: USGS: Mount Pocono, Pocono Pines

Finding the trailhead: From New York City drive west on Interstate 80 and cross the Delaware River on the I-80 bridge. Take exit 299 and drive north on Route 715 for 0.3 mile. Turn left at the stoplight onto Sullivan Road. (You are now between the Crossings Premium Outlet Mall and I-80. Be careful not to get on the I-80 on-ramp.) Drive 0.9 mile on Sullivan Road to a stop sign, and turn left onto Camelback Road. Drive 3.1 miles up the winding road to the State Game Lands 38 parking lot on your right. *DeLorme: Pennsylvania Atlas & Gazetteer:* Page 54 D1

The Hike

This hike starts out easy enough, and for the first 3.0 miles, it's a typical Pocono hike—plenty of rocks and brief ups and downs to a stunning high-altitude swamp and a glacial lake. But the final 1.2 miles is a very strenuous, steep climb up a very rocky power line right-of-way.

It's important for hikers to have an idea of what's involved in a hike: first to decide if they want to do it, and second to learn ahead of time what the challenges are. You would be well advised to wear sturdy hiking boots on this hike, especially for the final 1.2 miles. Also, if you plan to do this hike in hot weather, be sure to bring extra water for the final ascent.

This hike starts out on the access road to a number of radio and communications towers. These towers are surrounded by chain-link fences, and there is a concrete building at the base of each tower to encompass the necessary equipment. Still, it's something to see, and when you get back down from the mountain and are driving around, you can take a look up at Camelback Mountain and see if you can discern the towers.

▶ **The first heart-shaped tub to appear in the Poconos was at Ceasars Cove Haven in 1963.**

At 0.5 mile you come to a boulder with a sign that leads you first to Wolf Swamp and then to Deep Lake. Standing on the breastworks of the swamp, you are struck by the beauty of this swamp that looks more like a lake than a typical swamp. When you are on the breastworks, you can see a drainage pipe that feeds water from the swamp to the run-off stream, Wolf Swamp Run, which you will cross later in the hike.

Then it's up a short hill and back down into the forest on the trail that hikers share with horse and bicycle riders to the path near Deep Lake. This is one of those pristine glacial lakes that draw hikers, outdoors people, and photographers to the Poconos. While Wolf Swamp has an erratic shoreline, with coves and fingers of land that jut out into the water, Deep Lake looks perfectly round, and perfectly serene.

From the lake continue downhill until you reach the bottom of this ravine and cross over Wolf Swamp Run. From there it's on to an abandoned railroad grade that was once part of the Wilkes-Barre & Eastern Railroad. After that you're out of the trees and into the open swath of the power line. From here it's all uphill back to where you started.

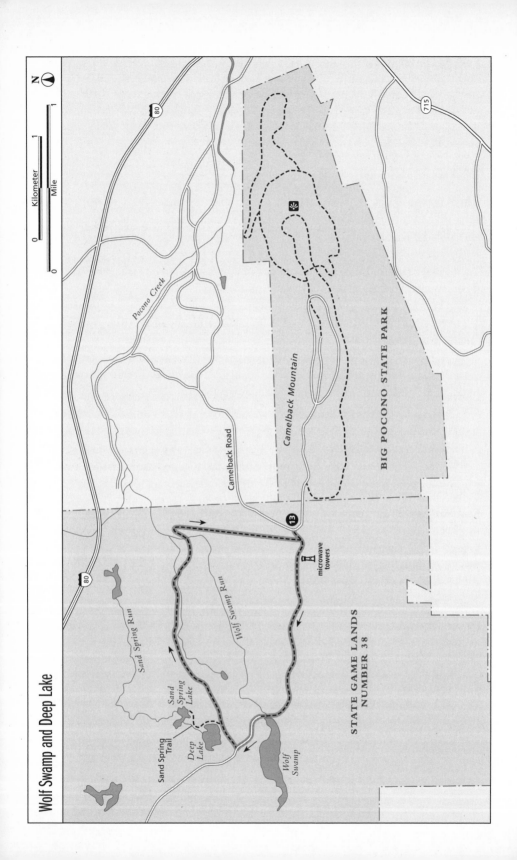

Wolf Swamp and Deep Lake

N

0   Kilometer   1

0   Mile   1

80

715

Pocono Creek

Camelback Road

Camelback Mountain

BIG POCONO STATE PARK

13

microwave towers

80

Sand Spring Run

Wolf Swamp Run

Sand Spring Trail

Sand Spring Lake

Deep Lake

Wolf Swamp

STATE GAME LANDS
NUMBER 38

Miles and Directions

0.0 Start at the State Game Lands 38 parking area. Walk to the metal gate, go around it, and continue on the dirt road. Pass the power line right-of-way, where you will return to this starting point. You will pass one radio tower on your right and then five more towers on your left.

0.2 Turn right onto a red-rock road.

0.5 Turn right at a large rock with a sign painted on it that reads WOLF SWAMP & DEEP LAKE.

1.2 Reach Wolf Swamp on your left. (**FYI:** Wolf Swamp looks more like a lake.)

1.4 Turn right at the Y intersection with a green triangle trail sign with a horse and a bicycle symbol. Walk about 100 feet and turn right onto the trail that goes by Deep Lake, which is on your left. (**FYI:** There are short trails along this section that lead down to the lake.)

1.5 Come to a Y intersection with a grassy trail on the left. Veer right at the Y and follow the green horse and bicycle trail sign. (**Option:** Follow the grassy trail north for a 0.6-mile round-trip to Sand Spring Lake.)

2.7 Turn right onto an abandoned railroad grade.

3.0 Turn right on a woods road that leads to the power line right-of-way; turn right at the power lines and head uphill.

4.2 Arrive back at the dirt road where you started, and turn left back to the parking lot.

4.3 Arrive back at the parking lot.

Options: Just past the eastern edge of Deep Lake, there is path that leads 0.3 mile to Sand Spring Lake, another glacial lake. If you chose to visit this lake, add 0.6 mile and another half hour to your overall hike.

If you don't think you can make the 1.2-mile ascent at the end of this hike, you can hike to Sand Spring Lake and simply return the way you came in, for a total of 3.6 miles. Either way, the scenery on this trail makes it a must-do hike.

Hike Information

Local Information
Pocono Mountains Visitors Bureau: 1004 Main Street, Stroudsburg; (570) 421-5791 or (800) 762-6667; www.800poconos.com

Local Events/Attractions
Pocono State Craft Festival: August, Quiet Valley Living Historical Farm, Quiet Valley Road, Hamilton Township; (570) 476-4460; www.poconocrafts.com
Stroud Mansion and Library: 900 Main Street, Stroudsburg; (570) 421-7703; http://mcha-pa.org

Accommodations
Meadowbrook Inn & Restaurant: Cherry Lane Road, Tannersville; (570) 629-8800; www.meadow brookinn.net
Pocono Vacation Park: Shafer School House Road, Stroudsburg; (570) 424-2587; www.pocono vacationpark.com

Restaurants
Food Court, Premium Crossings Outlet Mall: 1000 Route 611, Tannersville; (570) 629-4650

Organizations
Pocono Outdoor Club: www.poconooutdoorclub.org

Local Outdoor Retailers
Dunkleberger's Sports Outfitters: 585 Main Street, Stroudsburg; (570) 421-7950
Wal-Mart: 355 Lincoln Avenue, East Stroudsburg; (570) 424-8415

Even a trail sign hand painted on a boulder is better than no sign at all.

TANNERSVILLE CRANBERRY BOG

Even in an outdoor environment as unique as the Pocono Plateau, there are individual ecosystems here that are more unusual than what you might run into on a regular hike or outing. One such place is the Tannersville Cranberry Bog.

First off, the bog is named Cranberry not because it resembles a commercial cranberry bog but because Cranberry Creek originates in its northern marshy area. Cranberry Creek runs through the bog and then empties into Pocono Creek, which meanders along Interstate 80 into Broadhead Creek, which empties into the Delaware River.

There are cranberry bushes in the bog, but the cranberry is not the predominate feature of the bog. That title goes to the sphagnum moss, also called peat moss. What happened here in Tannersville is that over thousands of years, the moss filled in a kettle lake that was created during the last ice age.

The moss makes the water acidic and oxygen poor. This in turn inhibits decomposition and creates an environment where the only plant species that grow are those that can thrive in a nutrient-poor environment. That's what makes the plant life here rare and in some cases unique.

Two of the more unusual plants here are the sundew and the pitcher plant. Because the soil doesn't provide enough nutrients to sustain them, they have become carnivores—trapping and devouring insects that are attracted to their flowers.

There are other rare species here, such as twayblade and rose pogonia orchids, bog rosemary, Labrador tea, and cotton grass. Visitors might also catch a glimpse of the endangered bog turtle, a river otter, or a bobcat.

The bog is managed by the Monroe County Conservation District Environmental Educational Center. If you want to hike in here, you must call ahead and make an appointment with a guide/naturalist, who will lead the bog walk. There are also regularly scheduled tours. Call the MCCD at (570) 629-3061 or visit www.mcconserva tion.org for more information.

14 Big Pocono State Park

Hikers get ready to do the South Trail, which, as the sign points out, is open to equestrians and mountain bikers.

Local hikers say the view from this hike is the best in the Poconos. The mountain path is rocky in sections, with odd boulder formations. Once through the rocky section, you come to a flat, grassy area for the sweeping view and then loop back to the mountaintop for three more vistas.

Start: Parking Area 1, near the restrooms and the Cattell Cabin
County: Monroe
Nearest town: East Stroudsburg
Distance: 4.1-mile loop
Approximate hiking time: 3 hours
Difficulty rating: Moderate
Terrain: Rocky forest footpath
Elevation gain: 420 feet
Land status: State park
Other trail users: Hunters (in season)

Canine compatibility: Leashed dogs permitted
Fees/permits: No fees or permits required
Schedule: Year-round; caution advised during hunting seasons
Trail contacts: Big Pocono State Park, Tannersville, c/o Tobyhanna State Park, Tobyhanna; (570) 894-8336; www.dcnr.state .pa.us/stateParks/parks/bigpocono.aspx
Maps: USGS: Mount Pocono; Big Pocono State Park map

Finding the trailhead: From Sharon get on Interstate 80 at exit 4 and drive east 295 miles to exit 299. Turn left onto Route 715 and drive north for 0.3 mile to the stoplight. Turn left at the stoplight onto Sullivan Road. (You are now between the Crossings Premium Outlet Mall and I-80. Be careful not to get on the I-80 on-ramp.) Drive 0.9 mile on Sullivan Road to a stop sign. Turn left at the stop sign onto Camelback Road and drive 4.2 miles up the winding road. Continue straight at the park gate to Parking Area 1 near the Cattell Cabin. *DeLorme: Pennsylvania Atlas & Gazetteer:* Page 54 D1

The Hike

Big Pocono State Park is located at the very top of Camelback Mountain (elevation 1,566 feet.) While Camelback's elevation is less than half that of the highest point in the state (Mount Davis, at 3,213 feet above sea level), it feels higher simply because it's so steep. It is the mountain's sheer drop that gets your attention.

Our hike starts at Parking Area 1 in the center of the park. This is where you'll find the bulletin boards, restrooms, picnic areas, fire tower, heliport, tourist overlooks, and the stone cabin that was once used as park headquarters.

This core area is on a paved and mostly level plateau. To begin this hike, you walk along this plateau to the trail sign at 1.0 mile. From there you drop down the south face of the mountain to 1.2 miles, where the trail quits going downhill and traverses the side of the mountain on a wide, well-groomed trail much like any other trail you're likely to find in the Poconos.

At about 2.7 miles you pick up the Indian Trail, and from there to the overlook at 3.2 miles, the trail is rocky. Also in this 0.5-mile stretch are a number of odd rock formations, some of them the size of a small house. If you hike enough in Pennsylvania, you'll see other rock formations like these. When Mother Nature heaved these rocks and boulders skyward through the surface of the mountain, they came out in a willy-nilly fashion and have remained there ever since.

The vista—located on a flat, grassy spot high above the treetops—is well worth your effort. Many experienced local hikers consider this the best view in the Poconos. From the vista the trail loops around back to Rim Road, which you cross as you make your way through a small woods and back to your vehicle.

There are three other overlooks up here that you can visit. These overlooks are pointed out clearly on the park map. Once you're back at your vehicle and have taken your restroom, food, and water breaks, you can walk to these overlooks. If you don't have the energy left to walk, you can drive to the overlooks along Rim Road.

The hardest part of this hike was driving up the windy road and watching the gas gauge go down as we went up. In other words, you've already spent your money on the gas to get up here, so you might as well get your money's worth before heading back down.

While you're making your way along Rim Road, you can also visit the parking area above the ski slopes and get an idea of what it would be like to strap on a pair of skis and fling yourself down the side of a very steep slope. There is also a restaurant

Big Pocono State Park

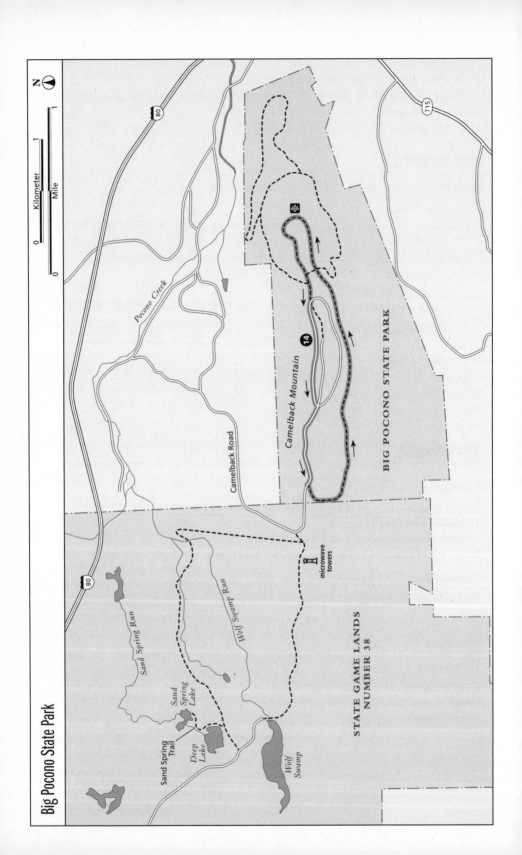

14

Camelback Mountain

Camelback Road

Pocono Creek

Sand Spring Run

Wolf Swamp Run

Sand Spring Lake

Sand Spring Trail

Deep Lake

Wolf Swamp

microwave towers

BIG POCONO STATE PARK

STATE GAME LANDS
NUMBER 38

80

80

715

N

Kilometer
0   1

Mile
0   1

here—the Cameltop—which has high, wide windows and an open deck that affords a panoramic view of the skiing area.

Warm weather visitors who don't hike or don't care to drive to the summit arrive at the restaurant via a chairlift. It's a hair-raising ride up, a burger, then a ride back down. In winter, of course, you ride the lift up and then ski back down.

Miles and Directions

0.0 Start at the parking lot by the Cattell Cabin. Walk back the way you drove in.

0.5 Pass through the park's main gate.

1.0 Turn left at the trail sign and walk between two boulders. Look for a yellow blaze on one of the boulders.

1.2 Arrive at a trail intersection and turn left onto the yellow-blazed South Trail.

2.0 Come to a South Trail signpost. The Vista Trail comes in from your left. Continue straight on the South Trail.

2.7 Arrive at a trail intersection. Go straight onto the orange-blazed Indian Trail.

3.2 Arrive at the vista area.

3.4 Come to a boulder in an open area, and turn right.

3.6 Pass the intersection with the Indian Trail. Continue straight.

3.7 Pass the intersection with the North Trail on your right. Continue straight.

3.8 Cross Rim Road and continue on the trail past a drinking fountain and a picnic area.

4.1 Arrive back at the parking lot.

Hike Information

Local Information
Pocono Mountains Visitors Bureau: 1004 Main Street, Stroudsburg; (570) 421-5791 or (800) 762-6667; www.800poconos.com
Twenty-four-hour fall foliage/ski hotline: seasonal; (570) 421-5565
Tourist information and free brochures: (570) 424-6050 or (800) 763-6667

Local Events/Attractions
Pocono Bazaar flea market: weekends, Marshalls Creek; (570) 223-8640; www.poconobazaar .com
Pocono Blues Festival: July, Lake Harmony; (570) 722-0100; www.jfbb.com/summer-blues -festival.asp

Accommodations
Mountaintop Lodge: Route 940, Pocono Pines; (877) 646-6636; www.mountaintoplodge.com
Mount Pocono Campgrounds: 30 Edgewood Road, Mount Pocono; (570) 839-7233; www.mt poconocampground.com

Restaurants

Barley Creek Brewing Company: Sullivan Trail and Camelback Road, Tannersville; (570) 629-9399; www.barleycreek.com

Organizations

Pocono Outdoor Club: www.poconoooutdoor.club
Susquehanna Trailers Hiking Club: www.susquehanna_trailers.tripod.com

Local Outdoor Retailers

Dunkleberger's Sports Outfitters: 585 Main Street, Stroudsburg; (570) 421-7950
Wal-Mart: 355 Lincoln Avenue, East Stroudsburg; (570) 424-8415

Sections of the trail are rocky, rocky, rocky.

15 Tobyhanna State Park

Look for Indian pipes along the trail.

This trail would make a great family hike. It's flat, and it passes through a magnificent forest of pine plantations and rhododendron patches as it loops around one of the prettiest lakes in the Poconos. There are picnic tables along the trail, and once back at the start, you have the swimming beach, a bathhouse, and more picnic tables.

Start: Parking Area 3
County: Monroe, Wayne
Nearest town: East Stroudsburg
Distance: 5.2-mile loop
Approximate hiking time: 2.5 hours
Difficulty rating: Easy
Terrain: Lakeside path, abandoned woods road, gravel road
Elevation gain: 80 feet
Land status: State park
Other trail users: Hunters (in season), anglers, bicyclists, snowmobilers and cross-country skiers (winter)
Canine compatibility: Leashed dogs permitted
Fees/permits: No fees or permits required
Schedule: Year-round; caution advised during hunting seasons. Snowmobilers use this trail in winter.
Trail contacts: Tobyhanna State Park, Tobyhanna; (570) 894-8336; www.dcnr.state .pa.us/stateParks/parks/tobyhanna.aspx
Maps: USGS: Tobyhanna; Tobyhanna State Park map

Finding the trailhead: From State College drive north on Route 26 and get on Interstate 80 at exit 16. Drive east on I-80 for 132 miles and take exit 293 to Interstate 380. Drive north on I-380 for 8 miles and take exit 8. Turn right onto Route 423 and drive north 2.5 miles to the park entrance on your left. *DeLorme: Pennsylvania Atlas & Gazetteer:* Page 53 C7

The Hike

If you came to the Poconos looking for a site to take postcard photos, Tobyhanna State Park should be at the top of your list. In fact, a few areas along the first 0.5 mile of this trail are so strikingly beautiful—with bushes and trees in the forefront and the lake as a backdrop—they appear to be landscaped. They're not.

The trail is essentially flat and starts out on a wide gravel path. If you're toting a hundred pounds of camera gear, you won't have to lug it up the side of a mountain to get a great shot.

At 0.9 mile you reach the dam, which has a special hikers' bridge over the spillway. Just beyond the dam you enter the forest and walk right into a rhododendron patch on both sides of the trail. Rhododendrons usually bloom in Pennsylvania in late June, but this can vary according to the weather. If you want to do this hike when they are in bloom, call the park environmentalist and check when conditions would be the best.

Shortly beyond the rhododendron, you pass through a pine forest. From there the forest is mostly made up of American beech, red maple, and many species of oak.

The forest trail is well groomed and well marked. Along the way you pass a series of mile markers. These are used in winter by snowmobilers, who ride the trail in the opposite direction as our hike. These mile markers have no bearing on our hike.

At 3.1 miles you come to stream named Pole Bridge Run. The pole bridge is gone. In its place the earth has been built up. Along each side of this buildup is concrete work that supports the buildup and houses the plastic pipes for the water to run through. At 4.0 miles you arrive at a major trail intersection. From there you cross over the tail end of the lake on a vehicle bridge. For the last section of the hike, you follow the blue blazes closer to the lake and back to where you started.

The lands around Tobyhanna and Gouldsboro Lakes have had a long and illustrious career. Starting in the early 1900s, ice was harvested from the lakes, stored in large barnlike structures, and then shipped on railcars to cities along the East Coast, where it was used for home iceboxes as well as for hospitals and hotels and other businesses that needed to keep their products chilled. During their heyday area ice plants shipped as many as 150 railcars of ice a day; but by the mid-1930s the ice industry slipped away as more and more people bought electric refrigerators.

In 1912 the U.S. Army chose the site that is now Tobyhanna and Gouldsboro State Parks as an artillery training camp. Over the years leading up to the Great Depression, which began in 1929, the base had been home to tank and ambulance training units. In the 1930s the site became one of Pennsylvania's Civilian Conservation Corps camps, which continued until 1937.

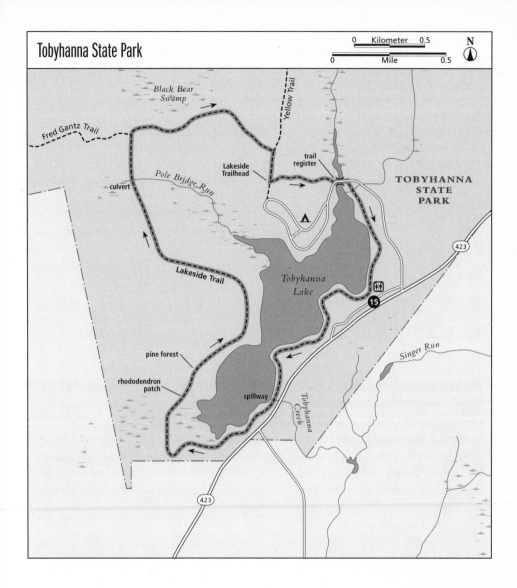

Black Bear
Swamp

Fred Gantz Trail

Yellow Trail

trail
register

Lakeside
Trailhead

Pole Bridge Run

culvert

TOBYHANNA
STATE
PARK

423

Lakeside Trail

Tobyhanna
Lake

15

pine forest

Singer Run

rhododendron
patch

spillway

Tobyhanna
Creek

423

0   Kilometer   0.5

0   Mile   0.5

N

From 1937 to 1941 the camp was used by West Point Military Academy to train its cadets in field artillery. During World War II German prisoners of war were held here. After the war, the land—by this time 26,000 acres—was acquired by the Commonwealth and was divided into Tobyhanna Army Depot, which still operates today; State Game Lands 127; and the two state parks: Tobyhanna, which opened in 1949, and Gouldsboro, which opened in 1958.

Miles and Directions

0.0 Start at Parking Area 3. Walk toward the bathhouse and the hand pump. Turn left at the hand pump and walk toward the blue blazes on the trees.

0.1 Come to double blue blazes and turn right. Come to a Y; continue straight toward the lake and get on the gravel trail.

0.5 Arrive at a picnic area, and walk toward the boat rental building.

0.6 Come to the boat launch and double blue blazes on the boat launch sign.

0.9 Arrive at the dam. Follow the blue blazes to a footbridge just below the spillway.

1.2 Turn right and head back into the forest. Pass a restroom, parking area, and picnic pavilion on your left.

1.6 Pass through a rhododendron patch and a pine forest.

2.3 The trail turns left, away from the lake.

3.1 Cross Pole Bridge Run on a culvert.

3.4 Come to the intersection with the red-blazed Frank Gantz Trail. Turn right and follow the blue blazes.

4.0 Come to an intersection with the Yellow Trail. Turn right and follow the blue blazes. Arrive at the Lakeside trailhead and turn left.

Fishing on Tobyhanna Lake.

THE WALKING PURCHASE OF 1737

What we now call the Poconos was originally home to the Delaware, Iroquois, Shawnee, Minisink, and Paupack Indians. When the first wave of Europeans came to settle the New World—then primarily the lands along the mid-Atlantic coast—William Penn soon realized that even though King Charles II had granted him a great deal of land, he would have to make peace and learn to coexist with the Native Americans.

Penn made treaties and purchased land from the Indians, even though Native Americans had no concept of private ownership of the land. They considered themselves descendants of the Great Spirit and that the land, like the air and forests, belonged to them as part of their heritage as the chosen people.

When Penn's sons inherited the colony's proprietorship, things started going badly. They soon found themselves in debt and in need of a new source of income. Settlers were moving westward, and land was at a premium. In addition, the provincial authorities needed to set up a government in the Delaware and Lehigh River Valley, and before they could do that, they felt they needed clear title to these lands.

At this point Thomas Penn and acting governor James Logan concocted a plan to divvy up the land. They convinced the Indians that the new government would take only the land that a white man could walk in eighteen hours and that all the land beyond that would belong to the Indians.

The deal was struck, but what the Indian leaders didn't know was that in preparation for the hike, Penn had sent men to clear a trail so that the men making the hike could cover more ground. If that weren't underhanded enough, he hired three experienced outdoorsmen to make the hike.

The amount of land Penn and Logan got was more than three times as much as the Indians had bargained for. It was now clear to the Indian leaders that these two men had disavowed William Penn's doctrine of treating everyone—including the Indians—fairly.

The white man got what he wanted: The land stretched from what is now Jim Thorpe to Lackawaxen and completely encompassed the land the Indians called the Minisink Territory. The Walking Purchase also set in motion an era of bloody warfare, complete with murderous raids, burned homes, and destroyed crops, that would continue for many years.

4.3 Arrive at a trail register by a yellow gate and Parking Area 5. Turn left onto the macadam road, and cross the bridge over the tail end of the lake.

4.6 Follow the blue blazes onto a shale road.

4.9 Pass a snowmobile trail on your left.

5.2 Arrive back at the bathhouse.

Hike Information

Local Information

Pocono Mountains Visitors Bureau: 1004 Main Street, Stroudsburg; (570) 421-5791 or (800) 762-6667; www.800poconos.com

Local Events/Attractions

Antique Co-op: Olde Engine Works Market Place, 62 North Third Street, Stroudsburg; (570) 421-4340; www.oldengineworks.com

Pocono Peddlers Village: Route 611 at Stadden Road, Tannersville; (570) 629-6366

Accommodations

Cranberry Manor Bed and Breakfast: 114 Cherry Lane Road, Tannersville; (570) 620-2246; www .cranberrymanor.com

Tobyhanna State Park Campground: Tobyhanna; (570) 894-8336 or (888) 693-9391 (for state-wide reservations)

Restaurants

Hazzard's Raintree Restaurant: 570 South Sterling Road (Route 191), South Sterling; (570) 676-5090

Organizations

Pocono Outdoor Club: www.poconooutdoorclub.org
Susquehanna Trailers Hiking Club: www.susquehanna_trailers.tripod.com

Local Outdoor Retailers

Dunkleberger's Sports Outfitters: 585 Main Street, Stroudsburg; (570) 421-7950
Wal-Mart: 355 Lincoln Avenue, East Stroudsburg; (570) 424-8415

16 Gouldsboro State Park

The trail passes through a diverse ecosystem—from ferns to boulder outcrops to a swamp.

You start this hike near the shore of Gouldsboro Lake; pick up the rocky Prospect Rock Trail that leads you first to Prospect Rock, an interesting rock outcrop; then it's downhill to a swampy area. Once through the swamp you get on a decommissioned highway that leads to a park road that delivers you back to the lake.

Start: Parking Area 1 off State Park Road
County: Monroe, Wayne
Distance: 5.6-mile loop
Approximate hiking time: 3 hours
Difficulty rating: Moderate, due to a short, steep, rocky climb
Terrain: Forest footpath, rocky footpath, swamp area, abandoned macadam road
Elevation gain: 300 feet
Land status: State park
Nearest town: East Stroudsburg
Other trail users: Hunters (in season),

bicyclists, cross-country skiers
Canine compatibility: Leashed dogs permitted
Fees/permits: No fees or permits required
Schedule: Year-round; caution advised during hunting seasons
Trail contact: Tobyhanna and Gouldsboro State Parks, Tobyhanna; (570) 894-8336; www.dcnr .state.pa.us/stateParks/parks/tobyhanna .aspx; www.dcnr.state.pa.us/stateParks/parks/ gouldsboro.aspx
Maps: USGS: Tobyhanna; Gouldsboro State Park map

Finding the trailhead: From Philadelphia drive north on Interstate 476 approximately 95 miles and get on Interstate 80 heading east. Drive east on I-80 for 19 miles and take exit 293 to Interstate 380. Drive north on I-380 for 13 miles to exit 13. Turn right onto Route 507 and drive east for 2 miles. Turn right into the park on State Park Road and continue approximately 2 miles to Parking Area 1 on your left. *DeLorme: Pennsylvania Atlas & Gazetteer: Page 53 C7*

The Hike

Gouldsboro State Park lies adjacent to and just west of Tobyhanna State Park. The parks are more or less divided by a single north–south railroad line that was once part of the Erie-Lackawanna Railroad. The nearby town of Gouldsboro and the park are named after Jay Gould, a nineteenth-century American entrepreneur and railroad tycoon who once owned nearly 10 percent of all the rail lines in the United States, including the Erie Railroad.

Gould used his rail lines to transport hides from the western United States and Australia to his nearby rail depots. From there he transported the hides by wagon nearly 10 miles on a plank road to the village of Thornhurst, where he had a leather tannery.

But it appears that early in his career, Gould got a little greedy and hatched a scheme to corner the market on gold and increase business on his railroads. His plan was that if he had all the gold, gold prices would go up and the price for other commodities—including wheat—would go up as well. This surge in wheat prices would give midwestern wheat farmers enough profit that they could afford to ship their wheat to the East—using Gould's railroads of course.

Gould's scheme caused gold prices to plummet, creating the stock market debacle of 1869 that become known as Black Friday. For his efforts Gould was besieged by lawsuits, lost his reputation, and was eventually forced out of the railroad business. Apparently undaunted by his troubles, he went on to own much of Western Union telegraph company and later was heavily involved in the elevated trains in New York City.

Tourist excursion train rides run through the park on the old Erie-Lackawanna line. These four-hour round-trip rides start at Steamtown National Historic Site in downtown Scranton and end at the restored 1908 Tobyhanna passenger and freight depot just outside the park on Route 423 in the village of Tobyhanna.

This hike—the Prospect Rock Trail—starts off easy enough on a well-marked, well-kept footpath through a forest that provides deep shade. But all that ends once you cross the park road at 0.9 mile and begin your trek over a rocky section that includes a steep, rocky climb to Prospect Rock. The rocks continue until about 2.2 miles, when the trail turns right onto an abandoned road.

From the right turn continue through Yetter Swamp. There is a bridge over the inlet stream, but depending on the season and the weather, you still may get a little muddy. On the other hand, if you do this hike after a dry spell, you'll hardly notice the swamp. From the bridge it's a short hike to Old Route 611, which was decommissioned in the 1970s and replaced by I-380.

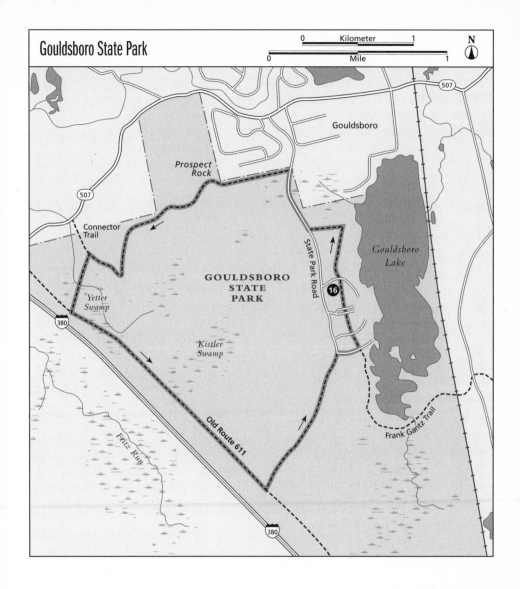

0 Kilometer 1

0 Mile 1

N

Gouldsboro

507

Prospect
Rock

507

Connector
Trail

State Park Road

Gouldsboro
Lake

16

GOULDSBORO
STATE
PARK

Yetter
Swamp

380

Kistler
Swamp

Old Route 611

Fritz Run

Frank Gantz Trail

380

You walk on Old Route 611 for about 1.2 miles. Old Route 611 continues south about another 1.5 miles to the park boundary. As you can imagine, the entire road is an ideal site for cross-country skiing. From the park boundary, Route 611 continues south and is a major north–south highway running through the heart of the Poconos and continuing south to Philadelphia.

At the old park entrance, turn left and head back toward Gouldsboro Lake. At 5.2 miles you arrive at the intersection with the Frank Gantz Trail; turn left here and follow the blue blazes back to Parking Area 1.

Miles and Directions

0.0 Start at Parking Area 1. Walk around the gate toward the lake. Pass the restrooms on your left and arrive at a bulletin board that reads PARKING AREA NO. 1. Turn left and follow the blue blazes.

0.3 The trail turns left, away from the lake.

0.5 Cross State Park Road and turn right.

0.9 Turn left into the forest at the double blue blazes on the back of a speed-limit sign.

1.3 Reach Prospect Rock. Descend north from the flat area, and turn left onto the trail.

2.2 The trail turns right.

2.5 Come to an intersection with the red-blazed Connector Trail. Turn left and follow the blue blazes.

2.6 Cross an inlet stream and pass through Yetter Swamp.

2.8 Reach Old Route 611 and turn left.

4.2 Turn left at the sign that reads OLD ENTRANCE ROAD.

5.0 Come to a gate and turn right onto the road heading toward the boat launch.

5.2 The Frank Gantz Trail comes in from your right. Turn left and follow the blue blazes.

5.6 Arrive back at Parking Area 1.

Hike Information

Local Information
Pocono Mountains Visitors Bureau: 1004 Main Street, Stroudsburg; (570) 421-5791 or (800) 762-6667; www.800poconos.com

Local Events/Attractions
Museum of the American Patriot: Grange Road (between Routes 611 and 940), Mount Pocono; (570) 839-1680

Tannersville Bog Walk: Monroe County Conservation District Environmental Center, 8050 Running Valley Road, Stroudsburg; (570) 629-3061; www.mcconservation.org

Accommodations
Meadowbrook Inn & Restaurant: Cherry Lane Road, Tannersville; (570) 629-8800; www.meadow brookinn.net

Tobyhanna State Park Campground: Tobyhanna; (570) 894-8336 or (888) 693-9391 (for state-wide reservations)

Restaurants
The Blakeslee Inn: Route 940, Blakeslee; (570) 646-1100; www.blakesleeinn.com

Organizations

Susquehanna Trailers Hiking Club: www.susquehanna_trailers.tripod.com
Pocono Outdoor Club: www.poconooutdoorclub.org

Local Outdoor Retailers

Dunkleberger's Sports Outfitters: 585 Main Street, Stroudsburg; (570) 421-7950
Wal-Mart: 355 Lincoln Avenue, East Stroudsburg; (570) 424-8415

Part of this hike includes Old Route 611, which was abandoned when Interstate 380 opened.

17 Hickory Run Boulder Field

The boulder field is 400 feet wide and 1,800 feet long. Some boulders are 25 feet long.

Don't visit the Poconos without doing this hike. First of all, any of the hikes in Hickory Run State Park are well worth doing simply because they take you through a pristine forest laced with clear mountain streams that make you wonder what life was like back when water from these streams ran the local mills. Second, this hike follows a meadow path and abandoned forest roads through a pine forest to the Hickory Run Boulder Field, the only natural phenomenon of this type east of the Mississippi. Bring your children and your camera.

Start: Boulder Field trailhead parking lot on the north side of Route 534 just east of Interstate 476

County: Carbon

Nearest town: Wilkes-Barre

Distance: 7.0 miles out and back

Approximate hiking time: 3.5 to 4.0 hours

Difficulty rating: Easy; mostly flat trail

Terrain: Meadow path, abandoned forest roads, boulder field

Elevation gain: 550 feet

Land status: State park

Other trail users: Tourists, hunters (in season)

Canine compatibility: Leashed dogs permitted

Fees/permits: No fees or permits required

Schedule: Year-round; caution advised during hunting seasons

Trail contacts: Hickory Run State Park, White Haven; (570) 443-0400; www.dcnr.state .pa.us/stateparks/parks/hickoryrun.aspx **Maps:** USGS: Blakeslee, Hickory Run

Finding the trailhead: From Wilkes-Barre drive south on I-476 and take exit 95 to Interstate 80. Go west on I-80 to exit 274 (first exit). Turn left onto Route 534, and drive south for 1.8 miles to the town of Lehigh Tannery. Turn left at the stop sign in town, and drive east on Route 534 for about 4 miles into Hickory Run State Park. Drive past the park office and continue about 4 miles until you pass under I-476. Park on the left, immediately after the underpass. *DeLorme: Pennsylvania Atlas & Gazetteer:* Page 53 D5

The Hike

At 15,500 acres, Hickory Run is one of Pennsylvania's largest state parks. It's also one of the most picturesque. Its forests are a mixture of second-growth white pine and hemlock, mixed oak, and northern hardwoods. Sand Spring Lake, the largest of the four impoundments in the park, has a swimming beach. Two clear mountain streams, Sand and Hickory Runs, intersect in the center of the park, at the site where a booming nineteenth-century logging mill and village once stood. A few of the village buildings remain and are used by the state park service; one is the park office. From March to November park environmental education specialists can help you fully appreciate the natural beauty of the park through hands-on activities, guided walks, and presentations on natural and historical resources.

▶ **In 1829 Anthony Dutot opened the first boarding house in the Poconos in the village of Delaware Water Gap.**

For hikers there's a 40-mile network of well-maintained trails leading through dense mountain laurel and rhododendron patches, along the pristine streams to dams and rustic spillways, and through to scenic areas like the Shades of Death Trail. Early settlers named the trail because the dense forests of virgin white pine and hemlock were so thick they blocked the sun from reaching the forest floor. But for many the major attraction in Hickory Run State Park is the Hickory Run Boulder Field—a geological formation of boulders created during the Pleistocene epoch or, as it's commonly called, the last ice age.

The term *Pleistocene* is derived from the Greek words *pleistos* (most) and *kainos* (recent), and scientists who have studied the boulder field believe it was created 15,000 years ago as a result of the same glacial activity that created North America's Great Lakes.

During the Pleistocene epoch, which began about 1.8 million years ago and ended about 10,000 years ago, huge ice sheets covered most of the earth. In North America the most recent ice sheet—the Wisconsin—stretched across most of the northern United States, creating a climate similar to that of present-day Greenland.

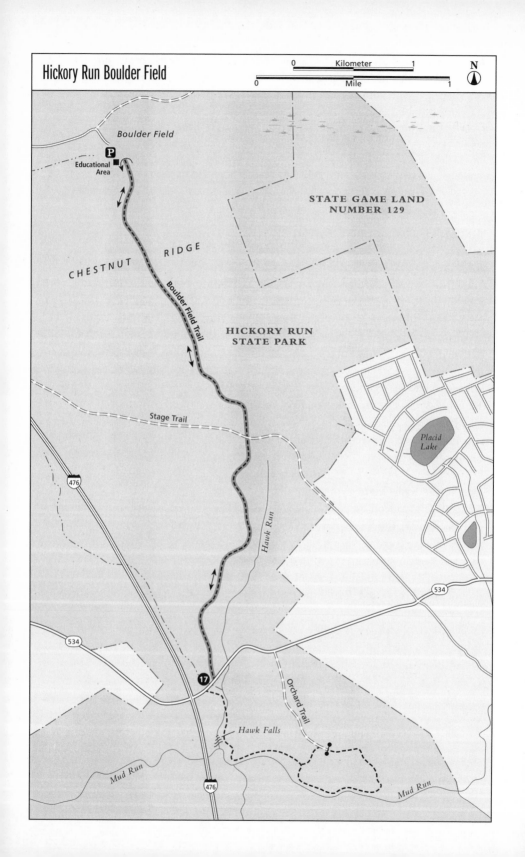

0   Kilometer   1

0   Mile   1

N

Boulder Field

P

Educational
Area

STATE GAME LAND
NUMBER 129

CHESTNUT   RIDGE

Boulder Field Trail

HICKORY RUN
STATE PARK

Placid
Lake

Stage Trail

476

Hawk Run

534

534

17

Orchard Trail

Hawk Falls

Mud Run

476

Mud Run

This ice sheet reached its southernmost point in northeastern Pennsylvania, about 1 mile north and 1 mile east of the boulder field.

When the sheet retreated, it left behind a moraine—an accumulation of boulders, stones, and debris. Meltwater from the glacier produced a freeze-thaw cycle that heaved the earth and split the cap rocks. This action, repeated over thousands of years, carried the rocks and boulders farther and farther downslope until the cycle stopped 15,000 years ago. The boulders' rough edges were rounded as they shifted. The resulting fine gravel, clay, and sand deposited around the boulders were washed away by glacial meltwater.

▶ **Lehigh comes from the German *lecha*, which is derived from the Native American word *lechauwekind*, meaning "where there are forks."**

Because there is no soil around the boulders, the field is more or less devoid of vegetation. But with every passing year, the red maple, alder, hemlock, and spruce that surround the field drop their foliage and contribute to humus capable of supporting small plants and saplings.

The boulders, which are red sandstone at the north end and red conglomerate with white quartz pebbles in the south end, vary in size from 4 to 25 feet in length. The field is 400 feet wide on an east–west axis and 1,800 feet long north to south. It's remarkably level and at least 12 feet deep. There are holes, what geologists call reliefs, that look as though someone had fashioned the holes around giant bowls.

The hike to and from the field itself is a pleasant walk through a pine forest. At a little over 1.5 miles, you'll cross the Stage Trail, originally the stagecoach route that ran from Bethlehem to Wilkes-Barre and stopped at the once-bustling sawmill town of Saylorsville, just north of the center of the park.

Miles and Directions

0.0 Start at the trailhead parking lot on the north side of Route 534. Walk to the trail sign and a set of wooden steps and then onto a path through an open field.

0.1 Come to the Boulder Field Trail sign. Follow the yellow blazes.

0.8 Cross a washout stream.

1.7 Cross the Stage Trail.

3.4 Arrive at the boulder field. Walk across the field to the educational bulletin boards.

3.5 Arrive at the bulletin boards. Turn around to walk back to the trailhead.

5.3 Recross the Stage Trail.

7.0 Arrive back at the parking lot.

Hike Information

Local Information

Pocono Mountains Visitors Bureau: 1004 Main Street, Stroudsburg; (570) 421-5791 or (800) 762-6667; www.800poconos.com

Carbon County Tourist Promotion Agency: Jim Thorpe; (570) 325-3673

Local Events/Attractions

Jim Thorpe River Adventures: One Adventure Lane, Jim Thorpe; (800) 424-7238; www.jtraft.com

Lehigh Gorge Scenic Railway: Old Mauch Chunk National Historic District, Jim Thorpe; (570) 325-8485; www.lgsry.com

The Mauch Chunk Museum & Cultural Center: Jim Thorpe; (570) 325-9190; www.mauchchunk museum.com

Accommodations

The Inn at Jim Thorpe: 24 Broadway, Jim Thorpe; (800) 329-2599; www.innjt.com

Mary's Guesthouse: hostel oriented, family/group arrangements, 37 West Broadway, Jim Thorpe; (570) 325-5354; www.marysjimthorpe.com

Mauch Chunk Lake Park Campground: Jim Thorpe; (570) 325-3669

Restaurants

Antonio's Pizzeria: 43 West Broadway, Jim Thorpe; (570) 325-3679

Organizations

Pocono Outdoor Club: www.poconooutdoorclub.org

Local Outdoor Retailers

Blue Mountain Sports & Wear: 34 Susquehanna Street, Jim Thorpe; (570) 325-4421 or (800) 599-4421; www.bikejimthorpe.com

Dick's Sporting Goods: 479 Arena Hub Plaza, Wilkes-Barre; (570) 823-8288

Wal-Mart: 500 Route 940, Mount Pocono; (570) 895-4700

Wal-Mart: 2150 Wilkes-Barre Township Marketplace, Wilkes-Barre; (570) 821-6180

18 Hawk Falls

Hawk Falls.

This easy hike leads you through rhododendron patches that are so tall they form tunnels over the trail. From there you hike alongside a well-known trout stream, whose clear waters cascade from one rock ledge to the next and then widen into deep pools where anglers prefer to cast. When you reach Hawk Falls, there are a number of vantage points where you can view this unique, three-sided waterfall.

Start: Hawk Falls trailhead parking lot, on the south side of Route 534 just east of Interstate 476

County: Carbon

Nearest town: Wilkes-Barre

Distance: 3.1-mile loop

Approximate hiking time: 2.5 hours

Difficulty rating: Easy; mostly level trail with one short switchback climb

Terrain: Paved and forest roads, rhododendron "tunnels"

Elevation gain: 424 feet

Land status: State park

Other trail users: Tourists, campers, anglers

Canine compatibility: Leashed dogs permitted

Fees/permits: No fees or permits required

Schedule: Year-round

Trail contacts: Hickory Run State Park, White Haven; (570) 443-0400; www.dcnr.state .pa.us/stateparks/parks/hickoryrun.aspx

Maps: USGS: Blakeslee, Hickory Run

Finding the trailhead: From Wilkes-Barre drive south on I-476 and take exit 95 to Interstate 80. Go west on I-80 to exit 274 (first exit). Turn left onto Route 534, and drive south for 1.8 miles to the town of Lehigh Tannery. Turn left at the stop sign in town and drive east on Route 534 for about four miles into Hickory Run State Park. Drive past the park office and continue about 4 miles until you pass under I-476. Park on the right immediately after the underpass. *DeLorme: Pennsylvania Atlas & Gazetteer:* Page 53 D5

The Hike

There are two misnomers on this hike. First, the waters of Mud Run are astonishingly clear. Second, you won't see any hawks or other raptors diving for fish on Hawk Run or at Hawk Falls. The creek and the falls are named for the Hawk family that once owned the property on which the eponymous creek and falls are located.

Of the twenty-two trails in the 15,500-acre Hickory Run State Park, Hawk Falls is the most popular with both locals and tourists. Most hikers take the direct route from the parking lot, across Hawk Run, and on to the falls. Some may wander upstream along Mud Run for a ways and then return the way they came. Fishermen generally drive through the campground and park at the parking lot just before the closed access gate. This way they only have to carry their gear about 0.5 mile.

But fishermen and tourists miss the pine forest and thriving rhododendron tunnels. Rhododendrons, some as tall as 15 feet, line both sides of the forest road that leads into a pristine forest of pines, beech, maple, and oak to Mud Run. Mud Run is popular with fly fishermen angling for a chance to hook a native or brook trout. If you do this hike in fishing season, you'll almost certainly be able to watch a fly fisherman in waist-high boots wading into the stream and flicking his line about. He's aiming toward one of the deep, shaded pools where he's convinced an enormous cagey old trout is just waiting to take his fly.

There is one short switchback climb out of the steepest section of the ravine. Once you make the summit, the yellow-blazed trail divides: One branch continues across the plateau; the other turns left. Take the branch that turns left to descend the ravine and make your way back to Mud Run. Look for a sheared-off stump that is taller than you, marked with a yellow blaze. Back at the creek, it's a short side trek to Hawk Falls, at the juncture where Hawk Run empties into Mud Run, which continues west until it empties into the Lehigh River.

Aside from the wonders of nature, hikers on this trail can marvel at the wonders of man's ingenuity. When you're at Hawk Falls, you are almost directly under the I-476 bridge spanning this gorge. From this vantage point you have a clear view of the underside of the bridge, which is high enough and far enough away that there is no traffic noise in the gorge.

After visiting the falls the trail takes you out of the ravine bottom and onto a very short side trail where you can view Hawk Falls from above. From there the trail continues to Hawk Run, where, depending on the water level, you can either ford the creek on exposed rocks or simply wade through it.

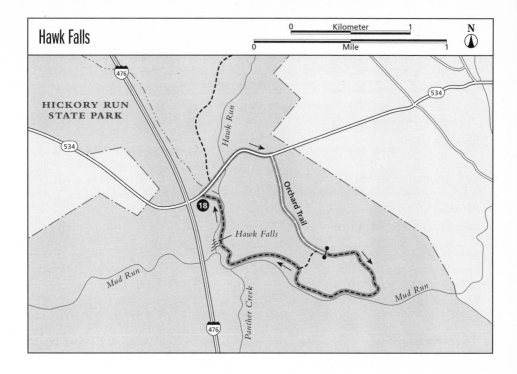

Hawk Falls

Wet feet or not, you are soon back to Route 534, where you turn right to return to your vehicle.

Miles and Directions

0.0 Start at the trailhead parking lot on Route 534. Walk east alongside the road.

0.1 Hawk Run passes under Route 534. Note the small dam on your left.

0.4 Turn right at the sign that reads Organized Group Camping onto the forest road. Follow the yellow blazes.

0.5 Pass restrooms on your right.

0.7 Pass another restroom on your right.

1.0 Come to an access gate across the road.

1.4 Pass an unmarked footpath on your right.

1.5 Turn right into a rhododendron tunnel.

1.6 Arrive at Mud Run and turn right.

2.0 The trail turns right to climb out of the ravine.

2.2 The trail turns left at the edge of the plateau. Turn left and begin your descent back down the ravine to Mud Run. Look for the yellow blaze on a large stump. (**FYI:** Another set of yellow blazes for the Orchard Trail continues across the plateau.)

2.5 Arrive at a trail intersection. Turn left and follow Mud Run to Hawk Falls.

2.6 Arrive at Hawk Falls. Retrace your steps back to the trail intersection.

2.7 Arrive at the trail intersection. Continue straight.

2.8 Turn left on a short side trail to an overlook above Hawk Falls. Retrace your steps back to the trail and turn left.

2.9 Ford Hawk Run.

3.1 Arrive at Route 534; turn right to the parking lot.

Hike Information

Local Information
Pocono Mountains Visitors Bureau: 1004 Main Street, Stroudsburg; (570) 421-5791 or (800) 762-6667; www.800poconos.com
Carbon County Tourist Promotion Agency: Jim Thorpe; (570) 325-3673

Local Events/Attractions
Steamtown National Historic Site: South Washington Avenue, Scranton; (570) 340-5200 or (888) 693-9391; www.nps.gov/stea
Electric City Trolley Station & Museum: Steamtown National Historic Site, South Washington Avenue, Scranton; (570) 963-6590; www.ectma.org/museum.html

Accommodations
Minnie Victoria Bed and Breakfast Inn: 732 North Street, Jim Thorpe; (570) 325-9992 or (866) 288-3229; www.theminnievictoria.com
Hickory Run State Park Campgrounds: White Haven; (570) 443-0400 or (888) 727-2757 (for statewide reservations)

Restaurants
Black Bread Cafe: 45–47 Race Street, Jim Thorpe; (570) 325-8957; www.blackbreadcafe.com

Organizations
Pocono Outdoor Club: www.poconooutdoorclub.org

Local Outdoor Retailers
Dick's Sporting Goods: 479 Arena Hub Plaza, Wilkes-Barre; (570) 823-8288
Wal-Mart: 500 Route 940, Mount Pocono; (570) 895-4700
Wal-Mart: 2150 Wilkes-Barre Township Marketplace Wilkes-Barre; (570) 821-6180

19 Beltzville State Park

Hikers enjoy the shade provided by a hemlock and mixed-hardwood forest.

You enter the forest on a pleasant, mowed path that leads you to a ravine alongside a stream. From there the trail leads you to the Wild Creek Falls area, where you can swim, eat your lunch on the flat boulders, or just watch as children splash about in the shallow water. The trail follows above Wild Creek as the stream makes its way to Beltzville Lake, where you get a view of the lake.

Start: Christman trailhead on Pohopoco Drive
County: Carbon
Nearest town: Allentown
Distance: 5.4-mile lollipop
Approximate hiking time: 3 hours
Difficulty rating: Moderate
Terrain: Grassy footpaths, forest roads, rocky footpaths
Elevation gain: 260 feet
Land status: State park

Other trail users: Hunters (in season), anglers
Canine compatibility: Leashed dogs permitted
Fees/permits: No fees or permits required
Schedule: Year-round; caution advised during hunting seasons
Trail contacts: Beltzville State Park, Lehighton; (610) 377-0045; www.dcnr.state.pa.us/stateparks/parks/beltzville.aspx
Maps: USGS: Palmerton; Beltzville State Park map and hiking trails brochure

Finding the trailhead: From Allentown drive north on Interstate 476 approximately 18 miles to exit 74 and U.S. Route 209. Turn right onto US 209 and drive south for 0.1 mile. Turn left onto Harrity Road and continue another 0.1 mile. Turn right onto Pohopoco Drive and continue for 6.4 miles to the Christman Trail sign and parking area on your right. *DeLorme: Pennsylvania Atlas & Gazetteer:* Page 67 B6

The Hike

Beltzville State Park comprises 2,972 acres that stretch along both sides of 949-acre Beltsville Lake, which sits on a southwest to northeast axis with the dam on the very southwestern tip. There are trails by the dam and on the southern side of the lake. Our hike is located in the northeastern section of the park and connects a number of short trails. (You can pick up a copy of the park map and hiking trails brochure at the park office, located near the dam.)

This hike starts out on a mowed path that connects with a forest footpath and an abandoned road. At a little over 1.0 mile, you arrive at the Wild Creek Falls area, where two major waterfalls send water cascading over stream boulders into a deep pool. This is a great spot to eat your lunch and watch as children splash around in the frigid water while other visitors toss sticks into the pool for their dogs to retrieve. Incidentally, you will return to the falls area, so you can eat your lunch either at the start or at the 4.3-mile point after completing most of the hike.

The hike pulls away from the falls and leads you up a ridge that runs parallel to Wild Creek to a point where the stream becomes an inlet of Beltzville Lake. From this vantage point you can see the lake and hear the motorboats cruising along. The trail runs as close to the lake as possible and then turns north, making a loop to return to the falls area.

If you're interested in the history of the early eastern United States, you can check out the two Sawmill Run hikes located near the dam. Many eastern U.S. settlements and towns were established near a stream that provided power to operate a mill. A dam was built to collect the water and then send it on its way through a millrace, where it powered a waterwheel that ran the mill. The mill at Beltzville was a gristmill. As you hike the trails, you can see the remains of the dam and the millrace. You can also see the remains of a 1700s-era slate quarry.

If you're looking for more to do after this hike, jump in your vehicle and follow US 209 west to the town of Jim Thorpe. Even though it's just 14 square miles and the population is a mere 4,892, Jim Thorpe (formerly called Mauch Chunk) is one of the most historically interesting sites in the state. It's fun, too.

The area rose to prominence with the discovery and mining of anthracite coal. From there it developed by creating strategies—such as barges and canals and railroads—to get the coal to the big cities, where it was used to create energy for manufacturing. When these industries declined after the Great Depression, the town survived by once again taking advantage of its natural resources—the Lehigh River

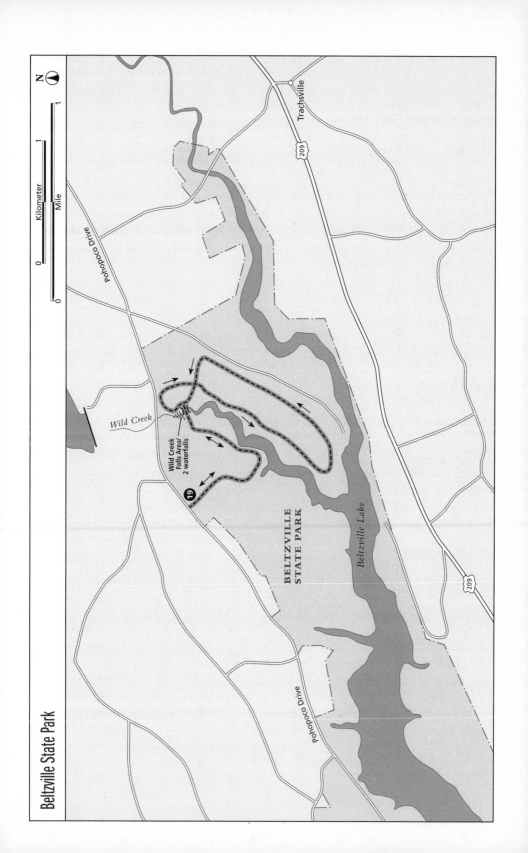

Beltzville State Park

and the steep and deep gorges that surround it—this time to establish itself as a tourist mecca, with many of the links to its grand past still intact.

Miles and Directions

0.0 Start at the Christman Trail parking lot. Walk past the gate and follow the yellow blazes.

0.3 Turn right and head downhill on the green-blazed trail along the stream.

0.4 Turn left away from the stream and begin an uphill climb.

0.5 Turn right onto the yellow-blazed Christman Trail.

0.6 Turn left at the T intersection.

1.0 Turn right onto the blue-blazed Falls Trail. (**FYI:** This trail also has white blazes at this point.)

1.1 Arrive at Wild Creek and cross the stream on a footbridge. Turn left on the other side and arrive at Wild Creek Falls.

1.3 The trail turns right.

1.5 Arrive at a mowed swath and turn right to the trail intersection. Walk uphill and then turn left onto the white-blazed Cove Ridge Trail.

3.9 Arrive back at the mowed swath. Turn left and walk alongside the swath.

4.0 Turn right, walk 50 feet, and then turn right again onto the swath. Retrace your steps downhill to the trail intersection.

4.1 Turn left onto the blue- and white-blazed trail.

4.3 Turn right at the blue and white arrows. Cross the footbridge across Wild Creek and walk uphill.

4.4 Turn right onto the yellow-blazed Christman Trail.

4.6 Turn left at the double yellow blazes.

5.0 Turn right at the yellow arrow.

5.2 Turn right toward the parking area.

5.4 Arrive back the parking area.

Hike Information

Local Information
Pocono Mountains Visitors Bureau: 1004 Main Street, Stroudsburg; (570) 421-5791 or (800) 762-6667; www.800poconos.com
Carbon County Tourist Promotion Agency: Jim Thorpe; (570) 325-3673

Local Events/Attractions
Asa Packer Mansion: Old Mauch Chunk National Historic District, Jim Thorpe; (570) 325-3229; www.asapackermansion.com
Eckley Miners Village: Highland Road, Weatherly; (570) 636-2070; www.eckleyminers.org

Accommodations

Canalside Guest House: 103 Canal Street, Lehighton; (610) 377-5599; www.canalside.org
The Parsonage Bed and Breakfast: 61 West Broadway, Jim Thorpe; (570) 325-4462 or (800) 799-0244; www.theparsonagebandb.com
Mauch Chunk Lake Park: 625 Lentz Trail, Jim Thorpe; (570) 325-3669; www.carboncounty.com/park

Restaurants

Gallo's Pub & Grill at Flagstaff: 600 Flaggstaff Road, Jim Thorpe; (570) 325-4554
Café Origins: 107 Broadway, Jim Thorpe; (570) 325-8776; www.cafeorigins.com

Organizations

Allentown Hiking Club: www.allentownhikingclub.org
Pocono Outdoor Club: www.poconooutdoorclub.org

Local Outdoor Retailers

Lehigh Gorge Outpost: 7 Hazard Square, Jim Thorpe; (570) 325-9226
Wal-Mart: 1091 Millcreek Road, Allentown; (610) 530-1400

Children play in the shallow water above Wild Creek Falls.

Glen Onoko Falls Trail

On a hot day, Onoko Falls is the place to be.

If you like a challenge, you'll love this hike. It is a steep climb over washouts, rocks, ledges, and boulders; but when you reach the top, you are rewarded with a view of two awe-inspiring waterfalls—two of the best in the state. The return trip is on a forest path.

Start: Glen Onoko Falls parking area, off Front Street in Jim Thorpe
County: Carbon
Nearest town: Allentown
Distance: 2.1-mile loop
Approximate hiking time: 2 hours
Difficulty rating: Difficult
Terrain: Steep, rocky gorge, man-made rock steps, forest footpath
Elevation gain: 900 feet
Land status: State game lands

Other trail users: Hunters (in season), anglers
Canine compatibility: Leashed dogs permitted
Fees/permits: No fees or permits required
Schedule: Year-round; caution advised during hunting seasons
Trail contacts: Lehigh Gorge State Park, White Haven; (570) 443-0400; www.dcnr.state .pa.us/stateparks/parks/lehighgorge.aspx
Maps: USGS: Weatherly

Finding the trailhead: From Allentown drive north on Interstate 476 approximately 18 miles to exit 74 and U.S. Route 209. Turn left onto US 209 and drive south to Lehighton. Continue on US 209 to Jim Thorpe to the downtown stoplight by the train station. From this stoplight drive 0.3 mile. Turn right at the next stoplight onto Route 903 and the bridge that takes you across the Lehigh River. Continue for 3 blocks and look for the Glen Onoko sign on your left. Turn left at the sign; continue downhill and follow the access road for 1.6 miles to the Glen Onoko parking area. *DeLorme: Pennsylvania Atlas & Gazetteer:* Page 67 B4

The Hike

There are a few places in Pennsylvania where outdoor buffs can do just about anything they've got the energy for. The Lehigh Gorge–Jim Thorpe area is just such a place: There is Class III whitewater rafting and kayaking on the Lehigh River, bicycling on 25 miles of abandoned railroad grade that runs alongside the river, mountain biking in the steep and rugged terrain, fishing for stocked trout near the Francis E. Walter Dam, cross-country skiing and snowmobiling in winter, and of course hiking.

The centerpiece of the gorge is Lehigh Gorge State Park. The park comprises 4,548 acres that run along both sides of the Lehigh River, from the dam to the north to the village of Jim Thorpe at the park's southern tip.

The modern history of the area began with the discovery of anthracite coal in nearby Summit Hill in 1791. To get the coal to market, barges were floated down the Lehigh River through an elaborate system of locks and dams, and by the 1830s a 5-mile canal system was completed. Meanwhile, loggers were clear-cutting the hillsides of the giant white pines and hemlocks that were used for lumber. By the turn of the twentieth century, fires had wiped out the sawmills, severe flooding had leveled the dams, and the railroad had become the main method of hauling coal in the area.

▶ In 1900 Niagara Falls was the number-one tourist attraction in the United States. Jim Thorpe was second.

At this point local entrepreneurs decided to use the railroad to bring tourists into their newly built resort hotel in Glen Onoko.

They built the Hotel Wahneta and, in addition to offering tennis and ballroom dancing, they soon were leading tourists on the same hike that you will be taking.

While it may appear at first glance that the Glen Onoko Falls hike is in Lehigh Gorge State Park, it's not. It's on State Game Lands 141, which means that although the hike is well blazed, there is no ongoing trail maintenance. On certain stretches of the hike, you can use the rock steps that were originally built as part of the hotel's pathway. For other stretches—where there is evidence of flooding and washouts—you are left to follow the red blazes that are painted on trees and rocks. Nevertheless, this is a great hike. As you struggle onward and upward, you are rewarded over and over again with breathtaking waterfalls and, at one point, an overlook of the valley below.

The trail leads you to cross Glen Onoko Run two times, right at two small waterfalls. At 0.7 mile you reach the lower cascades of Chameleon Falls and then reach the 60-foot falls after a short uphill scramble. Because of the way the sunlight hits the water as it drops over the purplish-gray sandstone, the falls seem to change colors—like a chameleon—depending on the season, the weather, and the time of day.

From Chameleon Falls it's another uphill climb to Onoko Falls, which used to be called Cave Falls because hikers can get behind a veil of water and stand protected and dry, like in a cave, under the cliff. After the falls you face more climbing before the trail leads away from the stream and down the gorge to where you began.

Miles and Directions

0.0 Start at the Glen Onoko Falls parking lot. Walk to the bulletin board and descend the concrete steps next to it. At the bottom turn right and walk under the railroad bridge.

0.1 Turn right, away from the river, and begin climbing on a series of switchbacks.

0.2 The trail levels off and turns left.

0.3 Come to a small waterfall and cross Glen Onoko Run above it. Follow the red blazes.

0.4 Turn right and cross the stream at a second small waterfall.

0.7 Reach the lower section of Chameleon Falls. After you view this section, turn right, away from the stream, and follow the red blazes over a rough, steep area.

0.8 Reach Chameleon Falls. After you view the falls, follow the red blazes toward the cliff and turn right at the cliff.

0.9 Turn left onto rock steps. Follow the red blazes to the area above Chameleon Falls. Turn right and follow the red blazes that are painted on the rocks. (**Option:** Cross the stream here and follow a trail spur to a vista then retrace your steps back to the trail.)

1.0 Arrive at Onoko Falls. After viewing the falls turn right to steps and a switchback to the left that takes you to a fire ring. Turn right at the fire ring and follow the trail.

1.9 Turn left at a T intersection and retrace your original steps under the railroad bridge.

2.1 Arrive back at the parking area.

Hike Information

Local Information

Pocono Mountains Visitors Bureau: 1004 Main Street, Stroudsburg; (570) 421-5791 or (800) 762-6667; www.800poconos.com

Carbon County Tourist Promotion Agency: Jim Thorpe; (570) 325-3673

Local Events/Attractions

Lehigh Valley Sportsfest: July, Allentown; www.sportsfest.org

Lehigh Gorge Scenic Railway: Old Mauch Chunk National Historic District, Jim Thorpe; (570) 325-8485; www.lgsry.com

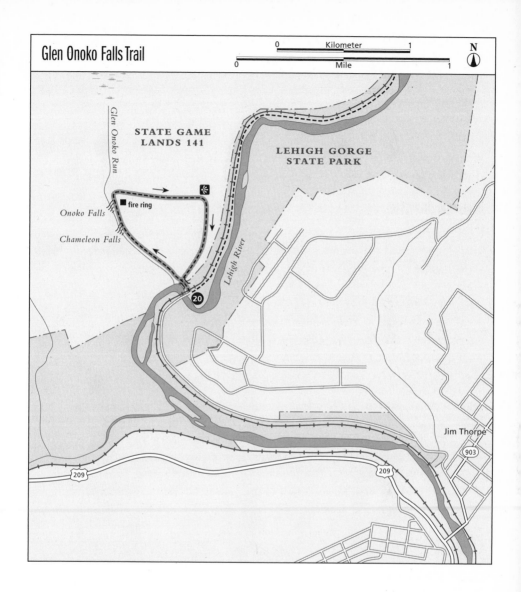

Accommodations

DeFeo's Manor at Opera House Square: Jim Thorpe; (570) 325-8777 or (888) 219-4036; www
.manorbedandbreakfast.com

Mary's Guesthouse: hostel oriented, family/group arrangements, 37 West Broadway, Jim Thorpe;
(570) 325-5354; www.marysjimthorpe.com

Jim Thorpe Camping Resort: 129 Lentz Trail, Jim Thorpe; (570) 325-2644; www.jimthorpecamping
.com

Restaurants

Fran's Covered Dish Cafe: 506 Center Street, Jim Thorpe; (570) 325-5566
Antonio's Pizzeria and Italian Restaurant: 43 West Broadway, Jim Thorpe; (570) 325-3679

Organizations

Allentown Hiking Club: www.allentownhikingclub.org
Pocono Outdoor Club: www.poconooutdoorclub.org

Local Outdoor Retailers

Blue Mountain Sports & Wear: 34 Susquehanna Street, Jim Thorpe; (570) 325-4421 or (800) 599-44121; www.bikejimthorpe.com
Wal-Mart: 1091 Millcreek Road, Allentown; (610) 530-1400

THE MOLLY MAGUIRES

Every town has in its past at least one major controversy that divided the residents back when it happened and continues to draw sides even today. More often than not, these controversies run along class lines: the haves against the have-nots. Put another way: Those who have control and wealth want things to stay the same; those on the bottom layer of society want things to change.

Such is the case of the Molly Maguires in the mines of the anthracite coal region. Most of these miners were Irish immigrants who had come to the United States to escape the potato famine. They also learned that working in the mines was not only dangerous but low paying, and many who worked for certain companies were not even getting money for their toil. They were paid in credit vouchers that they turned into the company for their rent and to buy items at the company store.

Talk of a union spread through the mines and made its way to the bosses. In response, Franklin Gowen, president of the Philadelphia and Reading Railroad, cut the miners' pay by 10 percent. The men went on a strike that lasted seven months. When they returned to work, Gowen cut their pay another 10 percent and things heated up. To quell the violence and silence the leaders, Gowen hired Pinkerton detectives, who went into the mines and worked as spies.

But the violence had begun. After several mine bosses were murdered, Gowen created his own private police force, which he called the Coal and Iron Police. Gowen's police arrested a number of miners that they claimed were the ringleaders and perpetrators of the murders and other violence. These men became known as the Molly Maguires.

After a trial in which Gowen served as one of the prosecutors and Pinkerton detective James McPharland provided much of the testimony, ten miners were found guilty and sentenced to death. On June 21, 1877, six men were hanged in Pottsville and four were hanged in Jim Thorpe, among them Alexander Campbell. Campbell was convicted of killing two mine bosses, but to the last he declared his innocence and on his way to the gallows he placed his hand on the wall of his cell and stated that his handprint would remain for all time to prove his innocence. His print is still on the wall of his cell and is a major tourist attraction.

Over the next two years, ten more men were found guilty and hanged. Despite his so-called victory Franklin Gowen became known as a greedy elitist and hanged himself in 1889. Today, historians are divided over the guilt or innocence of all the men that were hanged. Even though the Molly Maguires were short-lived, they began the movement that became one of the country's most powerful unions: the United Mine Workers.

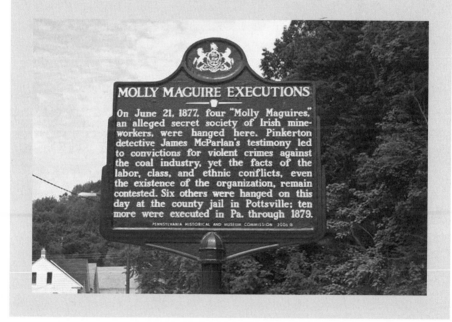

In Addition

Jim Thorpe: From Black Diamonds to Whitewater

The modern history of Jim Thorpe began in 1791 with the discovery of "black diamonds," aka anthracite coal, in nearby Summit Hill. The discovery couldn't have come at a better time: Coal from Jim Thorpe and the surrounding area would be used to fire up factories in places like Philadelphia and Baltimore, and these early manufacturers would spearhead the Industrial Revolution in the United States.

Of course in those days, Jim Thorpe was not Jim Thorpe. The town began its life as Mauch Chunk—a Lenni-Lenape Indian phrase meaning "Sleeping Bear Mountain." It wasn't until 163 years later that Mauch Chunk, like a Hollywood starlet, changed its name to Jim Thorpe. More about that later.

Seemingly overnight, the village was a regular boomtown, as hundreds of workers immigrated to town to work the mines. Meanwhile, a trio of entrepreneurs from Philadelphia got permission from the state legislature to try to make the Lehigh River more navigable so that they could float coal down the river to Easton, where they would meet the Delaware River and float on to their factory in Philadelphia.

In 1817 the trio, which had incorporated and become the Lehigh Coal and Navigation Company, took on their first project in Mauch Chunk. They immediately hired 500 men to build a road from the main mine at Summit Hill to Mauch Chunk, where coal was dumped into chutes and onto the scows that would float the coal to its destination.

Since the 9-mile run from the mine to the river was all downhill, the company came up with the idea of building a railroad of sorts to replace the coal wagons. Their idea was simple: They would let gravity do the work for them. They made up sections of coal cars and, with a brake operator on board, the cars ran down the rails. A separate train carried the mules down the hill so that they could pull the empty cars back up it, where the process would begin again.

Meanwhile, a series of canals had been completed, and in 1820 the company's first fleet of boats delivered 365 tons of coal to Philadelphia. The success of the company's endeavors spurned the growth of new industries and support business, such as mills, hotels, an iron-ore furnace, and even a few breweries.

By 1845 the teams of mules were set out to pasture or put to work in the mines as the company installed stationary steam engines to supply the power to return the empty cars up the hill. With the advent of stationary steam engines installed at different locations, more tracks were laid so that empty cars could return on a separate track. Other tracks were installed, and because at one location the drop was so steep, when they laid the tracks they laid them out using a series of switchbacks to slow the coal cars' descent. From then on, the rail system was referred to as the Switchback Gravity Railroad.

But Jim Thorpe's fortunes were about to be adjusted. During the mid-1800s a number of fires and floods destroyed businesses, homes, stores, and municipal buildings. Add to this the fact that railroads soon would become the dominant way to haul coal and other goods to market, and it's easy to see that the village needed to reinvent itself.

When the Switchback Gravity Railroad became obsolete, it was for a while opened to tourists to take a ride on the open cars. In fact, the open coal cars and the 9-mile drop became the prototype for a new American amusement: the roller coaster. These rides, one could say, were the village's first attempt to reinvent itself from an industrial town to a tourist town.

When Asa Packer came to town in 1851, he started the Lehigh Valley Railroad to haul coal and other goods from Mauch Chunk to Easton. In short order the village of Mauch Chunk once again became a boomtown as thousands of workers poured into the area to work on constructing Packer's railroad. The railroad boom in turn fostered a village-wide building boom that lasted for decades as workers replaced the buildings that had been destroyed in the earlier fires and floods.

By the end of the nineteenth century, Mauch Chunk, which now billed itself as the "Switzerland of America," was becoming known as a tourist mecca. Visitors came from all around to ride the Gravity Railroad, breathe in the clean mountain air, and eat and sleep in the newly built Victorian hotels that catered to their every wish.

Before he died in 1879, Packer had expanded the Lehigh Valley Railroad to 650 miles, from New York State to the New Jersey seaboard.

Mauch Chunk entered the twentieth century like most of the other towns in the area. It had the railroads, coal mines, and industry to keep its economy humming. But after the Great Depression of the 1930s, the area saw the decline of its two main industries: coal mining and railroads. As a result, many other businesses closed and the town began a long, slow decline as many of its workers left in search of greener pastures in the West or in larger cities.

By the 1950s town leaders were looking for a way to give the local tourist economy a shot in the arm. In 1953 Olympic athlete Jim Thorpe had died of cancer in a hospital charity ward in Philadelphia. Thorpe, widely regarded as the greatest athlete of the twentieth century, had fallen on hard times and was in fact penniless.

His widow, Patricia, who wanted a suitable monument created for him in his native Oklahoma, learned that Oklahoma would not contribute to a memorial in Thorpe's honor. Patricia Thorpe heard that Mauch Chunk and East Mauch Chunk were struggling to survive and that an editor for the *Mauch Chunk Times* named Joe Boyle had started an economic development fund by asking residents of the two towns to donate a nickel a week.

Patricia Thorpe visited Mauch Chunk and asked the town for assistance in establishing a monument for her husband. The town agreed. Thorpe's body was brought to town, and a granite mausoleum was erected in his honor along Route 903 on the east side of town. In 1954 the two towns of Mauch Chunk and East Mauch Chunk buried their rivalries and became a new town: Jim Thorpe.

Today Jim Thorpe is one of the most interesting and fun spots in Pennsylvania. Victorian structures—mostly homes turned into B&Bs, gift shops, restaurants, ice-cream shops, and bicycle and kayak rentals—line both sides of Main Street. You can walk or bicycle from one end of town to the other, visiting the Old Jail, the Opera House, or the historical churches with their spires pointing straight up. When you are hiking the surrounding mountainsides or visiting an overlook, the spires are like the needle of a compass, telling you where you are.

Beautiful, serene paths crisscross the Poconos.

21 Choke Creek Trail

Hikers make their way through tall grass and ferns undulating in the wind.

This is an easy hike through an open field of ferns and tall grass. You also pass through a section of rhododendron as you make your way to Choke Creek, a winding stream that is a favorite among fishermen and backpackers, who have set up a number of fishing spots and campsites beside the stream. If you need a little serenity, you'll find it here.

Start: Choke Creek trailhead on Tannery Road
County: Lackawanna
Nearest town: Scranton
Distance: 6.4-mile loop
Approximate hiking time: 3.5 to 4 hours
Difficulty rating: Easy
Terrain: Rocky footpath, grassy path, stream-side path, abandoned road, forest road
Elevation gain: 295 feet
Land status: State forest

Other trail users: Hunters (in season), backpackers, anglers
Canine compatibility: Leashed dogs permitted
Fees/permits: No fees or permits required
Schedule: Year-round; caution advised during hunting seasons
Trail contacts: Lackawanna State Forest, Scranton; (570) 963-4561; www.dcnr.state .pa.us/Forestry/stateforests/lackawanna.aspx
Maps: USGS: Thornhurst; Pinchot Trail System map

Finding the trailhead: From Easton drive north on Route 33 for approximately 25 miles to Interstate 80. Follow I-80 west for 18 miles to exit 284. Turn right onto Route 115 and drive north for 5.8 miles to River Road (State Route 2040). Turn right onto River Road and drive 4.9 miles to Bear Lake Road (State Route 2016). Turn left onto Bear Lake Road and drive 1.8 miles to Tannery Road (an improved dirt road) on your left. Turn left onto Tannery Road and drive 1.9 to the trailhead on your left. *DeLorme: Pennsylvania Atlas & Gazetteer:* Page 53 C5

The Hike

The Choke Creek Trail is part of the Pinchot Trail System, which is located within the boundaries of the 8,115-acre Lackawanna State Forest. The Pinchot Trail System is 23 miles of interconnecting loops, which (energetic) backpackers can do in one day or, as is more often the case, split the trail into two days of hiking and camping. Day hikers can carve out a loop that covers as much ground as they wish. The Choke Creek Trail is one of those carved-out trails.

There are two things you'll need on this hike: your camera and your lunch. Both hinge around Choke Creek—a pristine mountain stream that attracts brook trout fishermen and campers who just want to set up in a beautiful spot beside the stream.

About five minutes in, you pass through a major rhododendron patch that leads to an open area festooned with ferns and tall grasses that undulate in the breeze. From there it's on to Choke Creek, where you turn left and walk downstream. There are a number of small campsites along this section—mostly just fire rings and smootheddown earth that provide clues that campers have been here.

There are a number of small waterfalls along this section. At 3.7 miles you come to a deep pool in the stream where the water makes an abrupt right-hand turn and heads westward, away from where you're headed. Above the pool there is a flat boulder where you can stretch out and eat your lunch in the shade of a giant pine tree. This flat area has been used for camping, and it's easy to see why: It's high and dry, and it's the nicest spot on the whole trail.

After lunch follow the trail to its southwestern tip and then cut left and head northeasterly along the park border. Along this stretch you pass the Butler Trail and cross Butler Run. At this point the trail becomes the red-blazed Nature Trail. From there it's just 0.2 mile till you turn left onto a wide, grassy road that leads back to Tannery Road. When you drove in on this road, you probably didn't realize that it's a steady uphill climb. As you finish your hike on foot, it is quickly apparent that the last 0.6 mile back to the trailhead and your vehicle are all uphill.

If you drive out the way you came in, you'll pass the Bruce Swamp Natural Area on your left at Phelps Road, just a hair past where you hiked out onto Tannery Road. This eighty-seven-acre glacial bog swamp is shaped like a slice of pie, with Tannery Road as its base and Phelps Road and the Sunday Trail each making up a side that comes to a point.

Natural areas are unique scenic, geologic, or ecological sites that are maintained in their natural state so that physical and biological processes can occur with minimal

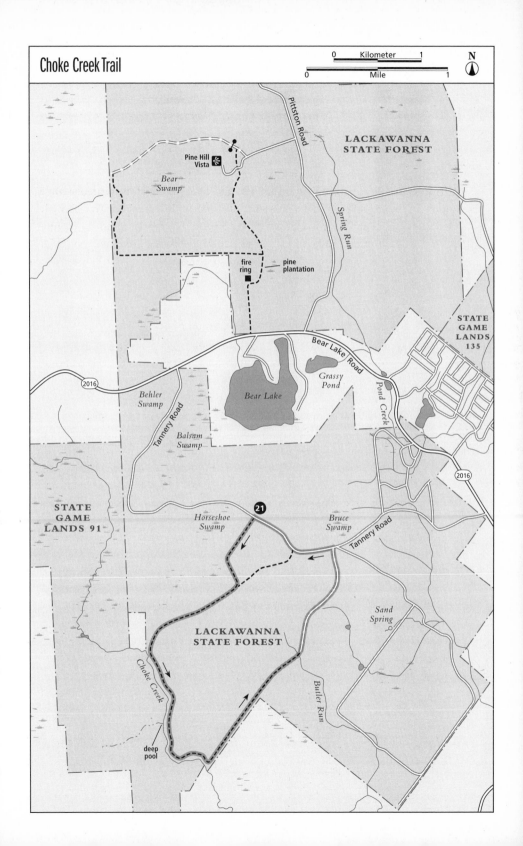

Choke Creek Trail

0 Kilometer 1

0 Mile 1

N

LACKAWANNA STATE FOREST

Pittston Road

Pine Hill Vista

Bear Swamp

Spring Run

fire ring

pine plantation

STATE GAME LANDS 135

Bear Lake Road

2016

Behler Swamp

Tannery Road

Bear Lake

Grassy Pond

Pond Creek

2016

Balsam Swamp

STATE GAME LANDS 91

Horseshoe Swamp

21

Bruce Swamp

Tannery Road

LACKAWANNA STATE FOREST

Sand Spring

Choke Creek

Butler Run

deep pool

interference from man. These areas are set aside for scientific study, to protect unique plant and animal communities, and to preserve areas of beauty and natural interest. Bruce Swamp, for example, is home to native spruce, balsam fir, and tamarack. It also supports Labrador tea and bog rosemary, species not normally found in Pennsylvania.

There are sixty-one state forest natural areas in Pennsylvania comprising 69,236 acres. The smallest of these is the ten-acre Box Huckleberry Natural Area in Perry County, just 2 miles south of New Bloomfield. At 16,433 acres, Bucktail State Park in Clinton and Cameron Counties is the largest. It runs from Lock Haven to Emporium.

From Bruce Swamp continue out on Tannery Road to Bear Lake Road (aka Bear Pond Road). Once on Bear Lake Road, turn right and retrace your route.

Miles and Directions

0.0 Start at the trailhead on Tannery Road. Follow the orange blazes.
0.4 The trail turns left.
0.8 Pass through a marshy area.
1.2 Cross a stream.
1.4 A trail goes off to your right. Turn left and continue to follow the orange blazes.
1.8 The trail veers left.
2.3 Turn left at Choke Creek. Pass a number of small campsites.
3.7 Come to a flat area and a deep pool.
3.8 The trail turns left at the private property line.
4.5 Pass the Butler Trail on your right. Continue straight and follow the red-blazed Nature Trail.
4.9 Cross Butler Run.
5.1 Turn left onto a grassy road.
5.8 Turn left onto Tannery Road.
6.4 Arrive back at the trailhead.

Hike Information

Local Information

Lackawanna County Convention & Visitors Bureau: 99 Glenmaura Boulevard, Scranton; (570) 963-6363 or (800) 22-WELCOME; www.visitnepa.org

Local Events/Attractions

Lackawanna Coal Mine Tour: 1 Bald Mountain Road, Scranton; (570) 963-6463 or (800) 238-7245; www.lackawannacounty.org/attractions_coal.asp
Everhart Museum: 1901 Mulberry Street, Scranton; (570) 346-7188; www.everhart-museum.org

Accommodations

Red Barn Village Bed and Breakfast: 1826 Red Barn Village, Clarks Summit; (800) 531-2567; www.redbarnvillage.com

Lackawanna State Park Campground: Dalton; (570) 586-0145 or (888) 727-2757 (for statewide reservations)

Restaurants

Russell's Restaurant: 1918 Ash Street, Scranton; (570) 961-8949

Organizations

Pocono Outdoor Club: www.poconooutdoorclub.org

Susquehanna Trailers Hiking Club: www.susquehanna_trailers.tripod.com

Local Outdoor Retailers

Dick's Sporting Goods: 600 Commerce Boulevard, Dickson City; (570) 963-1550

Gander Mountain: 955 Viewmont Drive, Dickson City; (570) 347-9077; www.gandermountain.com

The Choke Creek Trail passes through a major rhododendron patch.

22 Big Pine Hill

The Big Pine Hill hike begins at the Pinchot Trail System trailhead.

If you want to get away from civilization for a while, do this hike. You pass through a fragrant pine plantation as you make your way to an area that runs along a rocky ridge. From there you turn uphill for a sweeping view from the Pine Hill Vista tower. Hiking doesn't get any better than this.

Start: Pinchot Trail System trailhead on Bear Lake Road
County: Lackawanna
Nearest town: Scranton
Distance: 5.1-mile lollipop
Approximate hiking time: 2.5 hours
Difficulty rating: Easy
Terrain: Rocky, forest footpath; grassy road; dirt road
Elevation gain: 370 feet
Land status: State forest

Other trail users: Hunters (in season), backpackers
Canine compatibility: Leashed dogs permitted
Fees/permits: No fees or permits required
Schedule: Year-round; caution advised during hunting seasons
Trail contacts: Lackawanna State Forest, Scranton; (570) 963-4561; www.dcnr.state .pa.us/Forestry/stateforests/lackawanna.aspx
Maps: USGS: Pleasant View Summit; Pinchot Trail System map

Finding the trailhead: From Bloomsburg drive east on Interstate 80 for 52 miles to exit 284. Turn right onto Highway 115 and drive north for 5.8 miles to River Road. Turn right onto River Road and drive 4.9 miles to Bear Lake Road. Turn left onto Bear Lake Road and drive 4.2 miles to the trailhead and parking area on your right. *DeLorme: Pennsylvania Atlas & Gazetteer:* Page 53 C5

The Hike

This hike is in such a pretty spot that even the parking lot—with its overarching pines, rustic hand pump, and picnic pavilion—looks like a small park. The trails, which are blazed with rectangles—orange for secondary trails, red for the main trail—are very well maintained and well marked. The trail turns are also well marked with the standard double blazes.

The trail was laid out by a retired truck driver named Frank Gantz. If you hike around this area, you'll see his name on other hiking trails that he laid out. One connects the trails in Tobyhanna State Park with the trails in Gouldsboro State Park. Gantz laid out the Big Pine Hill Trail in 1975. The Youth Conservation Corps and the Sierra Club of Northeast Pennsylvania then built the trail, which was officially dedicated in 1982.

As soon as you get to the trail register, you see that this forest has a variety of plants and plenty of pine trees. Right away, you see sheep laurel, blueberries, teaberry, sassafras trees, spruce trees, and of course plenty of white pines, including an abandoned pine plantation. If you come here on a hot and sunny summer day and linger at the pine plantation, you can smell the fragrance of the pine trees in the air.

Just for practice, when you get to the Frank Gantz Trail sign at 0.8 mile, you can tie orange blazing tape on the sign so that when you return to this sign you'll know you're at the right place. This trail is so basic that the tape isn't really necessary, but it's a good habit to get into, especially if you're on a trail with the same type of sign at a number of different sites or on any other hike where you're trying to get back to where you started.

From the Frank Gantz Trail, turn right and head north along the White Line Trail, which runs along the border between Lackawanna and Luzerne Counties. It is also the western border of the Lackawanna State Forest. Leave the White Line Trail and hike 0.8 mile on a grassy road until you reach a forest service gate, where you turn right and reenter the forest and pass through a rocky area. All along this area you can see evidence of the power of Mother Nature as she heaved and forced giant boulders up out of the earth, creating a ledge that runs hundreds of feet alongside the trail. You leave this area and turn uphill for a short climb to the plateau at the top of Big Pine Hill.

Most hikers would agree that getting to a great vista usually entails a long and arduous climb. But on this hike things are different. You reach the Pine Hill Vista and its panoramic view with just a 0.2-mile uphill climb. If you look southeast from the viewing platform, you can see Bradys Lake—a long, thin lake that runs north to south on State Game Lands 127 off Highway 940.

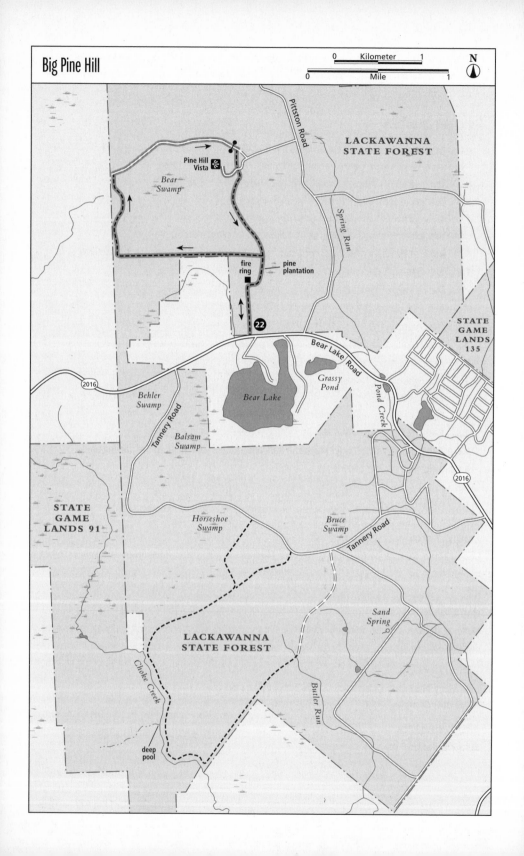

Big Pine Hill

Pittston Road

LACKAWANNA
STATE FOREST

Pine Hill
Vista

*Bear
Swamp*

Spring Run

fire
ring

pine
plantation

22

Bear Lake Road

STATE
GAME
LANDS
135

2016

*Behler
Swamp*

Tannery Road

Bear Lake

*Grassy
Pond*

Pond Creek

*Balsam
Swamp*

2016

STATE
GAME
LANDS 91

*Horseshoe
Swamp*

*Bruce
Swamp*

Tannery Road

*Sand
Spring*

LACKAWANNA
STATE FOREST

Choke Creek

Butler Run

deep
pool

After the view return to the trail and make your way back to the intersection with the Fred Gantz Trail, where we first began the loop. From there retrace your steps back to the parking lot.

Miles and Directions

0.0 Start at the parking lot and walk toward the trailhead sign and path. The trail begins with a short uphill climb. Follow the orange blazes of the Powder Magazine Trail.

0.2 The trail levels off on a plateau, and you arrive at the trail register.

0.4 The trail turns right at the double orange blazes. Pass a campfire ring on your left.

0.5 Arrive at the intersection of the Powder Magazine Trail and the red-blazed Pine Hill Trail. Turn left and follow the Pine Hill Trail. Pass a pine plantation on your right.

0.8 Arrive at the Frank Gantz Trail sign, and turn left onto the red-blazed Frank Gantz Trail.

1.8 Turn right onto the orange-blazed White Line Trail, and head north.

2.3 The trail turns right. Cross a swampy area on wooden planks.

2.5 Turn right onto a grassy road. Ignore a grassy road off to your left.

2.7 The Scrub Oak Trail goes off to your left. Continue straight.

2.8 A grassy road marked with snowmobile icons comes in from your right.

3.3 Arrive at a gate across the road. Turn right and enter the forest.

3.5 Turn right on the dirt road, and begin an uphill climb.

3.7 Arrive at the Pine Hill Vista platform. Retrace your steps back down to the trail and turn right.

4.3 Pass the Frank Gantz Trail on your right. Continue straight.

4.6 Turn right onto the Powder Magazine Trail, and retrace your steps to the parking area.

5.1 Arrive back at the parking area.

Hike Information

Local Information
Lackawanna County Convention & Visitors Bureau: 99 Glenmaura Boulevard, Scranton; (570) 963-6363 or (800) 22-WELCOME; www.visitnepa.org

Local Events/Attractions
Arts & Crafts Festival: October; Jack Frost Mountain, Blakeslee; (800) 468-2442; www.jfbb.com
Miller's Orchards Farm Market: 1515 Fairview Road, Clarks Summit; (570) 587-3399; www.millersorchard.com

Accommodations
Blueberry Mountain Inn B&B: Thomas Road, Blakeslee; (570) 646-7144
WT Family Camping: Route 115, Blakeslee; (570) 646-9255; www.wtfamily.com

Restaurants
Villa Virella: Olympia Lane, Blakeslee; (570) 646-3265

Organizations
Pocono Outdoor Club: www.poconooutdoorclub.org
Susquehanna Trailers Hiking Club: www.susquehanna_trailers.tripod.com

Local Outdoor Retailers
Dick's Sporting Goods: 600 Commerce Boulevard, Dickson City; (570) 963-1550
Gander Mountain: 955 Viewmont Drive, Dickson City; (570) 347-9077; www.gandermountain.com

The Poconos have more picturesque waterfalls than any other region in the state.

23 Frances Slocum State Park

The footbridge across Abrahams Creek sits high above the stream.

On this hike, just like many of the Pocono hikes, you'll come upon stone walls that outline an area that was once a farmer's field or a land boundary. In one area of this hike, you'll see an elaborate wall system unlike many of the others. The walls here were built to hold livestock, and this erstwhile landowner even built a dam to provide water for his livestock. This may be one of the most interesting hikes in the Poconos.

Start: Environmental Interpretive Center
County: Luzerne
Nearest town: Scranton
Distance: 3.8-mile lollipop
Approximate hiking time: 2 hours
Difficulty rating: Easy
Terrain: Grassy trail, lakeside trail, forest footpath, pine forest
Elevation gain: 220 feet
Land status: State park

Other trail users: Hunters (in season), fishermen
Canine compatibility: Leashed dogs permitted
Fees/permits: No fees or permits required
Schedule: Year-round; caution advised during hunting seasons
Trail contacts: Frances Slocum State Park, Wyoming; (570) 696-3525; www.dcnr.state.pa.us/stateParks/parks/francesslocum.aspx
Maps: USGS: Kingston; Frances Slocum State Park map

Finding the trailhead: From Harrisburg drive north on Interstate 81 approximately 100 miles to exit 165B (a left exit). Merge onto Route 309 and drive north for 7.2 miles. Turn right onto Carverton Road and continue for 4.2 miles. Turn left onto Eighth Street Road and continue for 1.3 miles. Turn left onto Mt. Olivet Road and drive for 1 mile. Turn left into the park entrance and drive 1 mile to a T intersection. Turn right and park on the left. *DeLorme: Pennsylvania Atlas & Gazetteer:* Page 52 B3

The Hike

This hike begins at the Environmental Interpretive Center. Facing the lake, turn right and pass through the picnic area, where you get your first view of Frances Slocum Lake. The 165-acre lake is shaped like a horseshoe, so at this point you are actually on a peninsula that juts out into the lake. The dam that created the lake was built to control flooding; picnicking areas were added and the park was officially opened to the public in 1968.

But in a few short years, the park was to become more than just a place to fish and roast hot dogs. From June 21 to June 23 in 1972, Tropical Storm Agnes ravaged the entire Atlantic Coast. The worst-hit area was the Susquehanna River basin. With its torrential rains, winds, and raging floodwaters, the storm caused $3.7 billion in damage as well as sixty-seven fatalities in the basin. The flooding in nearby Wyoming Valley was so severe that 280 families had to abandoned their homes and live in temporary residences in the park until their homes were restored to a livable condition. The park was reopened in 1974.

At the Deer Trail sign, walk on a mowed path into the forest, where you encounter a series of stone fences. At this point in the trail, you take the high road, which includes a short outer loop and then reconnects with the lower trail at the first wooden bridge.

After you cross the first bridge, the trail soon becomes a gravel road that leads to a first-rate bridge over Abrahams Creek. From there turn left onto a macadam road that was abandoned when the lake was created. This road runs 0.5 mile southeast straight into the lake; in the other direction it runs 0.2 mile northwest to the gate at the border of the park. A parking area just outside the park, across Mt. Olivet Road, is used by fishermen so that they can park there and walk directly to the lake.

While the road to nowhere essentially goes nowhere, it does take you through a picturesque marsh where the lake ends. Here you'll see, among the usual swampland suspects, pink swamp roses and the spotted, purple-pink joe-pye weed. The road really does take you into the marsh—literally: Water flows over the road, so intrepid hikers must take giant steps on about a dozen round concrete stepping-stones that, thankfully, keep your boots dry.

For the next segment of the hike, you cut uphill and enter a sort of netherworld of nineteenth-century stone walls, man-made stone steps that lead from the bottom of a rock outcrop to a flat area on the top, and the ruins of a stone dam. One theory

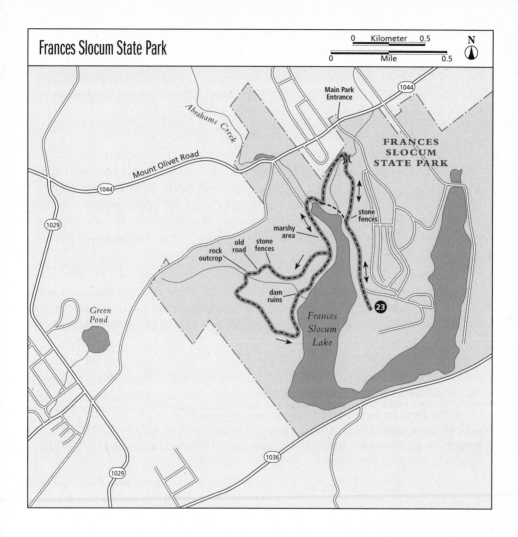

about this area is that farmers built the stone fences to corral their livestock and that the dam was built to provide water for farming and for the livestock.

After exploring the dark forest of the rock ruins, walk along the lakeside then emerge in the sunlight back onto the macadam road. From there retrace your steps back to the twenty-first century and the park.

Miles and Directions

0.0 Start at the Environmental Interpretive Center. Facing the lake, turn right and walk toward the Deer Trail sign.

0.1 Arrive at the Deer Trail trailhead. Follow the yellow blazes.

0.3 Arrive at a Y. Turn right and pass through a stone fence. Arrive at a second Y. Turn right and pass through a second stone fence.

0.5 Turn left at double yellow blazes and then jog right.

0.6 Cross a stream on a wooden bridge and turn left onto a grassy road.

0.8 Arrive at a Y. Turn left, go over a second wooden bridge, and then turn left onto an old macadam road.

1.0 Arrive at a marshy inlet. Walk on the round concrete stepping-stones.

1.3 Just before you reach the lake, turn right onto the trail and then turn right again at a second Y intersection. Follow the yellow blazes and pass through two stone fences.

1.5 Reach a third stone fence and bear left.

1.6 Arrive at an old road that has stone walls running along each side. Turn right onto the old road.

1.7 Turn right onto man-made stone steps that lead to the top of a rock outcrop. Turn left at the top then turn left again. Turn left again and descend toward the lake.

1.8 Turn left, cross a stream, and pass dam ruins on your left.

2.1 Turn left at the double yellow blazes. The blue-blazed trail continues straight. Cross two streams.

2.4 Pass a yellow-blazed trail on your left. Continue straight alongside the lake.

2.5 Turn left onto the old macadam road. Retrace your steps across the larger bridge and then cross the smaller bridge and turn right. Turn right again and retrace your steps back toward the trailhead.

3.8 Arrive back at the Environmental Interpretive Center.

Hike Information

Local Information
Luzerne County Convention and Visitors Bureau: 56 Public Square, Wilkes-Barre; (888) 905-2872; 145 East Broad Street, Hazleton; (800) 698-7111; www.tournepa.com

Local Events/Attractions
Northeast Fair: July; Pittston Township; (570) 654-2503; www.northeastfair.com
Canterbury Tours & Services: 51 Comstock Road, Tunkhannock; (570) 241-6807 or (800) 664-4714; www.canterburyts.com

Accommodations
Bischwind B&B: One Coach Road, Bear Creek; (570) 472-3820; www.bischwind.com
Frances Slocum State Park Campground: Wyoming; (570) 696-3525 or (888) 727-2757 (for statewide reservations)
Moon Lake County Park Campground: 196 Moonlake Road, Hunlock Creek; (570) 477-5467; www.moonlakepark.com

Restaurants
Cooper's Seafood Waterfront: 304 Kennedy Boulevard, Pittston; (570) 654-6883; www.coopers seafood.com

Organizations

Pocono Outdoor Club: www.poconooutdoorclub.org
Susquehanna Trailers Hiking Club: www.susquehanna_trailers.tripod.com

Local Outdoor Retailers

Dick's Sporting Goods: 600 Commerce Boulevard, Dickson City; (570) 963-1550
Gander Mountain: 955 Viewmont Drive, Dickson City; (570) 347-9077; www.gandermountain.com

FRANCES SLOCUM: THE LOST SISTER

Frances Slocum State Park is the only state park in Pennsylvania named for a woman. Her story begins in 1778 when a party of Lenni-Lenape Indians raided her family's home near Wilkes-Barre. Several family members were away from the house at the time, but her mother, sister, and one brother were there, as well as a boy who was living with the family.

The Indians took what they wanted from the house. They shot and killed the boy who was staying there. They grabbed Frances and her brother, but their older sister was able to get the brother free. Frances's mother never saw her again, but her brothers, who had vowed to find her, began a search that would last almost sixty years.

In 1838 word reached Joseph Slocum, who still lived in Wyoming Valley, that a white woman was living as the widow of a tribal chief near Peru, Indiana. Joseph traveled to the Indian village, and even though the woman no longer spoke English, they were able to confirm that she was his long-lost sister. Joseph tried to get her to return with him to his home but she refused, saying that she was no longer part of his world. She considered herself an Indian.

Frances had married two chiefs. Both had died, leaving her with two sons and two daughters. She told her brother that she was considered a queen among the Indians and would never leave the tract of land her relatives had secured for her. True to her word, Frances remained on the land till her death in 1847.

24 Nescopeck State Park

Part of the trail is an old service road that has turned to high grass.

Some state parks just seem so remote and out in the middle of nowhere that they're hard to resist. This newly refurbished state park is just such a spot. The trail here begins on a wide grassy road that leads to the banks of Nescopeck Creek, which is listed as a high-quality coldwater fishery. From there you go through a swamp and then on to Frances Lake. This is a great hike for children and a great place to spend a day.

Start: Parking area on Honey Hole Road
County: Luzerne
Nearest town: Wilkes-Barre
Distance: 3.7-mile lollipop
Approximate hiking time: 1.5 to 2 hours
Difficulty rating: Easy
Terrain: Grassy roads, lakeside footpaths, forest footpaths
Elevation gain: 165 feet
Land status: State park

Other trail users: Hunters (in season), anglers
Canine compatibility: Leashed dogs permitted
Fees/permits: No fees or permits required
Schedule: Year-round; caution advised during hunting seasons
Trail contacts: Nescopeck State Park, Drums; (570) 403-2006; www.dcnr.state.pa.us/stateparks/parks/nescopeck.aspx
Maps: USGS: Freeland, Whitehaven; Nescopeck State Park map

Finding the trailhead: From Bloomsburg drive east on Interstate 80 approximately 30 miles to exit 262. Turn right onto Route 309 and drive south for 0.75 mile. Turn left onto Honey Hole Road, and drive 5.2 miles to the parking area on your right. *DeLorme: Pennsylvania Atlas & Gazetteer:* Page 52 D4

The Hike

This is an easy hike that just about anyone could do. The majority of the hike is on an abandoned forest road that has turned into a wide, grassy footpath. When you do leave the main trail, you enter the forest on a typical forest footpath that gets you up close and personal with a huge beaver pond and then the nine-acre Lake Frances. There is also a section where the trail leads you through a deeply shaded pine forest.

At about 0.8 mile you begin to hear the faint rustling sounds of movement in the forest. At 0.9 mile you hear the unmistakable rush of the waters of Nescopeck Creek, which runs 6 miles through the park and then continues south and west until it joins Black Creek and empties into the North Branch of the Susquehanna River at the borough of Nescopeck.

At 0.9 mile a short fisherman's trail on your right leads to the banks of Nescopeck Creek. The creek—which is designated a high-quality coldwater fishery—is home to brown trout and native brook trout.

The trail passes through diverse ecosystems and wildlife habitats from wetlands to mixed hardwood forests. Just like most of the forests of Pennsylvania, the 3,550-acre park and the land surrounding it—State Game Lands 187—are home to gray squirrel, beaver, rabbit, white-tailed deer, turkey, and black bear. And there is one species of bird that you may see here that is not seen in other Pennsylvania forests: the American woodcock.

The woodcock, also known as the timberdoodle, is a shorebird that lives in the forests and farm fields and goes about its day probing the soil for its favorite food: invertebrates, especially earthworms. The woodcock, like its look-alikes the ruffed grouse and common snipe, is well camouflaged and is difficult to see sitting in its ground-based nest, which is often set in a small depression and surrounded by leaves. The best time to see a woodcock is at dusk when it goes out probing the earth with its extra-long, flexible bill that is sensitive to the movement of worms and other invertebrates in the soil.

If you visit the park during March or April, you can witness the timberdoodle mating ritual, which takes place each spring in the parking lot near the park office.

The state of Pennsylvania currently has 117 state parks. Nescopeck is one of its newest. The Commonwealth began buying properties for the park in 1971. Although the park was officially opened to the public in those days, there were no facilities in place until the park infrastructure was completed in 2001. In December 2002 construction began on the Raphael J. Musto Environmental Education and Visitors Center, which was completed in April 2004.

Today the center is host to a number of outdoor and environmental programs

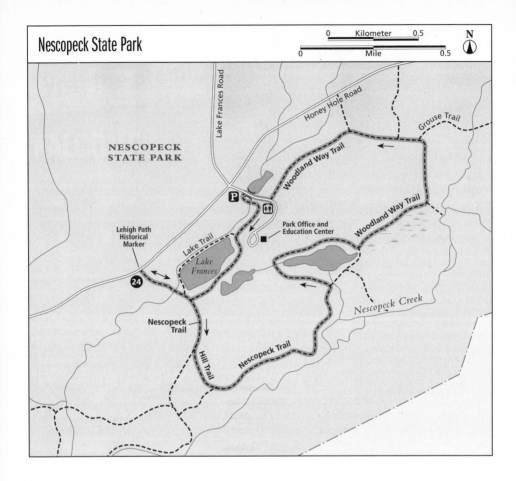

Nescopeck State Park

NESCOPECK
STATE PARK

Lake Frances Road

Honey Hole Road

Grouse Trail

Woodland Way Trail

Woodland Way Trail

Lehigh Path
Historical
Marker

Park Office and
Education Center

Lake Trail

Lake
Frances

24

Nescopeck
Trail

Nescopeck Creek

Hill Trail

Nescopeck Trail

0   Kilometer   0.5

0   Mile   0.5

N

aimed at students and the general public alike. Park personnel, along with the volunteer group Friends of the Nescopeck, conduct wildflower walks, canoe demonstrations, and fly-fishing and fly-tying demonstrations throughout the seasons.

When you combine the splendor of its new visitor center, lighted walkways, bridges, and paved parking lot with Lake Frances and Nescopeck Creek, the newly invigorated Nescopeck State Park is just simply a great place to spend a day.

Miles and Directions

0.0   Start at the parking area near the blue Pennsylvania Historical and Museum Commission sign that reads LEHIGH PATH. Walk around the metal gate. You are on the Nescopeck Trail.

0.2   Pass over two culverts through a swampy area.

0.3   Pass a trail sign on your left that reads To LAKE TRAIL AND LAKE PARKING.

0.4   Bear left at the Y intersection and get on the Hill Trail. The Nescopeck Trail goes to the right.

0.6 The Nescopeck Trail reconnects with the Hill Trail. Turn left and continue on the Nescopeck Trail.

0.8 Enter a pine forest.

0.9 Pass a fisherman's trail on your right that leads to Nescopeck Creek.

1.0 Come to a trail intersection and a sign for the Nescopeck Trail. Make a severe left turn and enter the forest. A pond is on your right.

1.4 Cross a seasonal stream. Turn right onto the Woodland Way Trail.

1.8 The trail turns left and uphill, away from the pond.

2.0 Turn left at a T intersection and continue on the Woodland Way Trail.

2.2 Pass the Grouse Trail on your right and then an unnamed trail on your right at the Honey Hole Road sign.

2.4 Pass another Honey Hole Road sign on your right. Turn left; continue on the Woodland Way Trail and enter a hemlock forest.

2.7 Turn right at the stop sign on the macadam road.

2.8 Cross the bridge over the stream that feeds Lake Frances. Arrive at the parking lot and turn left. Walk on the walkway to the far end of the parking lot.

3.0 Turn left at the Lake Trail sign. At the Y go left and enter the picnic area. Turn right on the Lake Trail and arrive at the head of Lake Frances.

3.2 Pass the outdoor amphitheater on your left.

3.3 Turn left at the sign that reads To The Nescopeck Trail.

3.4 Turn right onto the Nescopeck Trail.

3.7 Arrive back at the parking area.

Hike Information

Local Information
Carbon County Tourist Promotion Agency: Jim Thorpe; (570) 325-3673
Luzerne County Convention and Visitors Bureau: 56 Public Square, Wilkes-Barre; (888) 905-2872; 145 East Broad Street, Hazleton; (800) 698-7111; www.tournepa.com

Local Events/Attractions
Fine Arts Fiesta: May, Wilkes-Barre; www.fineartsfiesta.org
Oktoberfest at the Lion Brewery: October, North Pennsylvania Boulevard, Wilkes-Barre; (570) 823-8801; www.lionbrewery.com

Accommodations
The Sign of the Rose Bed and Breakfast: 501 South Franklin Street, Wilkes-Barre; (570) 824-1022 or (877) 767-3262; www.signoftherose.com
Lehigh Gorge Campground: Route 940, White Haven; (570) 443-9191; www.lehighgorgecampground.com

Restaurants
The Stage Coach Inn Restaurant: 668 North Hunter Highway, Drums; (570) 788-5158; www.stagecoachonline.com

Organizations

Pocono Outdoor Club: www.poconooutdoorclub.org
Susquehanna Trailers Hiking Club: www.susquehanna_trailers.tripod.com

Local Outdoor Retailers

Dick's Sporting Goods: 479 Arena Hub Plaza, Wilkes-Barre; (570) 823-8288
Wal-Mart: 2150 Wilkes Barre Township Marketplace, Wilkes-Barre; (570) 821-6180

Look for this historical marker beside the trailhead.

25 Ricketts Glen

Much of the Falls Trail consists of indigenous red-rock slabs placed alongside Kitchen Creek.

Hike through a natural area of 500-year-old trees and up a deep ravine on man-made stone steps. Walk alongside a raging mountain stream past more than two dozen wild and dramatic waterfalls. This is an extremely popular hike with tourists and photographers, so if you're a serious hiker and like to feel the serenity of the deep woods, you would do well to take this hike on a weekday.

Start: From the Ricketts Glen Natural Area parking lot on Route 118
County: Luzerne
Nearest town: Wilkes-Barre
Distance: 7.1-mile lollipop
Approximate hiking time: 5 hours
Difficulty rating: Moderate; extensive, steep climb and stone steps
Terrain: Well-worn forest path, shale walkways, dirt roads
Elevation gain: 1,081 feet
Land status: State park

Other trail users: Tourists
Canine compatibility: Leashed dogs permitted
Fees/permits: No fees or permits required
Schedule: Year-round
Trail contacts: Ricketts Glen State Park, Benton; (570) 477-5675; www.dcnr.state .pa.us/stateParks/parks/rickettsglen.aspx
Maps: USGS: Red Rock
Special considerations: Regardless of the season, the stone steps can be wet and slippery. Hiking boots with good tread are strongly advised. The weather in the ravine can

change abruptly—usually to a cold rain—so foul-weather gear is also recommended. On the plus side, take your swimming suit and water shoes: There are shallow pools where hikers can walk under the falls.

Because of the heights and the slippery stones and sometimes muddy and slippery trail, this hike is not recommended for those who are not physically fit.

Finding the trailhead: From Williamsport drive east on Interstate 180/U.S. Route 220 approximately 15 miles and take the US 220 exit. Continue on US 220 about 10 miles to Beech Glen and the intersection with Route 42. Turn right onto Route 42 south. Drive 4.5 miles and merge onto Route 239. Continue on Route 239 for 5.1 miles and merge onto Route 118 east. Continue on Route 118 for 12 miles, past the village of Red Rock and past the first Ricketts Glen State Park sign. Continue 2.3 miles on Route 118 to the Ricketts Glen sign and parking lot on your right. *DeLorme: Pennsylvania Atlas & Gazetteer:* Page 51 B7

The Hike

At Ricketts Glen history meets geology, and the result is a truly unique hike. This is not only the most magnificent hike in the state, but it also ranks up there with the top hikes in the East.

This hike has everything: It is a National Natural History Area, with trees estimated to be up to 900 years old. There are breathtaking waterfalls, pristine settings boasting unique flora and fauna, and mammoth trees strewn along the trail and across the creeks. Here at Ricketts Glen, even the drainage streams that pour into Kitchen Creek produce picture-postcard waterfalls.

Ricketts Glen State Park encompasses 13,050 acres along the Allegheny Front in Sullivan, Columbia, and Luzerne Counties. It's named for Colonel Robert Bruce Ricketts, a veteran of the Civil War who enlisted in the army as a private and after leading a battery of men at Gettysburg was awarded the rank of colonel upon his discharge. But Ricketts's greatest impact on this area was as a businessman, not a colonel. When the railroad reached the area, Ricketts began a major logging industry, at one point employing more than 1,000 men. To more easily move the massive logs, two lakes were built on the plateau above the glen; Lake Jean and Mountain Stream Lake still exist today. The 245-acre Lake Jean is used for recreation and fishing. The Pennsylvania Fish & Boat Commission owns Mountain Stream Lake and the land around it. It, too, is open for fishing.

Kitchen Creek drains Lake Jean and drops 1,000 feet down the ravine. A little over halfway down, it's joined by its eastern branch, which drains the other side of the ravine. Together they form the Y around which the hike is formed. You'll hike uphill along one branch and then downhill along the other.

The Glens Area is remote and is believed by scholars to be just as it was when Europeans first came to America. This remoteness has yielded an ecosystem free of introduced species. The glen is home to a wide variety of mosses and lichens; false nettle, also called bog hemp; ferns; and wild sarsaparilla, a member of the ginseng

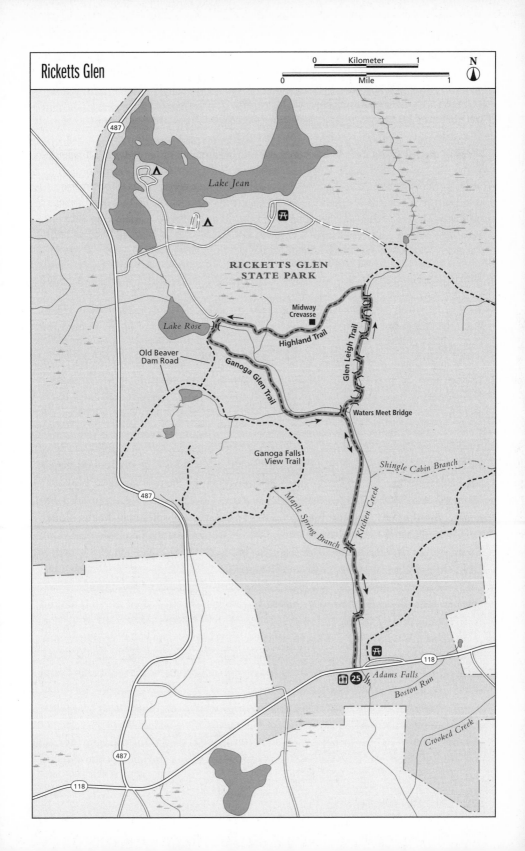

Ricketts Glen

0 Kilometer 1

0 Mile 1

N

Lake Jean

**RICKETTS GLEN
STATE PARK**

Midway
Crevasse

Highland Trail

Lake Rose

Glen Leigh Trail

Old Beaver
Dam Road

Ganoga Glen Trail

Waters Meet Bridge

Ganoga Falls
View Trail

Shingle Cabin Branch

Maple Spring Branch

Kitchen Creek

Adams Falls

25

Boston Run

Crooked Creek

487

118

family. Throughout this forest there are 100-foot-tall hemlocks and oaks boasting 5-foot diameters, as well as birch, ash, and striped maple. The trail itself is more than one hundred years old; workers employed by Ricketts built it to make a path along the falls. The trail is mostly placed stone steps that, because of the spray of the falls, can be wet and muddy even on a sunny day.

The forces of nature are hard at work in the glen. Huge fallen trees crisscross Kitchen Creek at every turn. A heavy rain sometimes obliterates steps. Walkways are frequently washed away. But the repair work is ongoing. There are a number of newly built bridges, and the entire walkway to Onondaga Falls, which was washed out during a storm, has been rebuilt.

Ricketts Glen is a haven for hikers, photographers, botanists, outdoor lovers, and tourists; it is not, however, suitable for small children. For those who can't make this hike, there is an excellent waterfall south of Route 118, adjacent to the parking lot. Adams Falls cascades 36 feet into a deep bowl formed by the shale bottom. The trail to it passes through a stand of picturesque pines, where there are picnic tables and benches.

Miles and Directions

0.0 Start at the parking area. Cross Route 118 at the crosswalk and walk to the trailhead and Glens Natural Area Falls Trail sign.

0.1 Arrive at the Falls Trail map and bulletin board.

0.2 Turn right onto a footbridge across Kitchen Creek.

0.3 Turn left onto a dirt road.

0.5 Cross a tributary on a footbridge. Arrive at a trail sign and turn right.

0.8 Turn left onto a footbridge and cross Kitchen Creek.

0.9 The trail veers left away from the creek. Look for the yellow-arrow signpost.

1.3 Arrive at Murray Reynolds Falls.

1.5 Arrive at Sheldon Reynolds Falls.

1.6 Arrive at Harrison Wright Falls.

1.8 Turn right onto Waters Meet Bridge and onto the Glen Leigh Trail.

1.9 Arrive at Wyandot Falls. Turn right onto the footbridge.

2.1 Arrive at B. Reynolds Falls. Turn left onto the footbridge and arrive at B. Ricketts Falls.

2.2 Arrive at Ozone Falls.

2.3 Turn right onto the footbridge and arrive at Huron Falls.

2.4 Arrive at Shawnee Falls.

2.6 Turn left onto the footbridge and arrive at F. L. Ricketts Falls. Climb the wooden steps.

2.7 Turn right onto the footbridge and arrive at Onondaga Falls.

2.8 Turn left onto a wooden bridge.

2.9 Cross a feeder stream.

3.0 Turn left onto the Highland Trail. Stay to the right at the trail fork.

3.4 Pass through Midway Crevasse.

4.0 Turn left onto the Ganoga Glen Trail.

4.2 Cross West Branch Kitchen Creek on a large wooden bridge. Pass the intersection with the Old Beaver Dam Road Trail. Turn left at the sign for Falls Trail and arrive at Mohawk Falls.

4.4 Arrive at Oneida Falls.

4.5 Arrive at Cayuga Falls.

4.6 Arrive at Ganoga Falls. Pass the Ganoga Falls View Trail on your right.

4.8 Arrive at Seneca Falls and Delaware Falls.

4.9 Arrive at Mohican Falls.

5.0 Arrive at Conestoga Falls.

5.2 Arrive at Tuscarora Falls and Erie Falls.

5.3 Arrive at the Waters Meet Bridge and retrace your steps toward Route 118.

7.1 Cross Route 118 to the parking lot and your vehicle.

Hike Information

Local Information
Luzerne County Convention and Visitors Bureau: 56 Public Square, Wilkes-Barre; (888) 905-2872; 145 East Broad Street, Hazleton; (800) 698-7111; www.tournepa.com

Local Events/Attractions
Nanticoke Music Fest: June, Nanticoke; (570) 735-2800; www.nanticokecity.com
Wilkes-Barre Triathlon: August, Wilkes-Barre; (570) 822-2025; www.wilkesbarretriathlon.com

Bus Service:
Fullington Trailways: Clearfield; (814) 765-7871 or (800) 942-8287. There is a bus stop in Red Rock, 1.25 miles west of the trailhead. The bus schedule dictates an overnight stay in the park. Since Red Rock is a flag stop, it's best to call Fullington for more information before traveling.

Accommodations
The Featherbed and Breakfast: 126 Jamison City Road, Benton; (570) 925-2277; www.feather bedandbreakfast.com
Ricketts Glen State Park: Benton; (570) 477-5675 or (888) 727-2757 (camping information and reservations)

Restaurants
Brass Pelican: 1119 Elk Grove Road, Benton; (570) 925-5425
Ricketts Glen Hotel: 221 Route 118, Benton, (570) 477-3656

Organizations
Pocono Outdoor Club: www.poconooutdoorclub.org
Susquehanna Trailers Hiking Club: www.susquehanna_trailers.tripod.com

Local Outdoor Retailers
D&R Sporting Goods: 620 Fairchild Street, Nanticoke; (570) 735-1480
Dick's Sporting Goods: 479 Arena Hub Plaza, Wilkes-Barre; (570) 823-8288
Wal-Mart: 2150 Wilkes Barre Township Marketplace, Wilkes-Barre; (570) 821-6180

The Art of Hiking

When standing nose to nose with a mountain lion, you're probably not too concerned with the issue of ethical behavior in the wild. No doubt you're just terrified. But let's be honest. How often are you nose to nose with a mountain lion? For most of us, a hike into the "wild" means loading up the SUV with expensive gear and driving to a toileted trailhead. Sure, you can mourn how civilized we've become—how GPS units have replaced natural instinct and Gore-Tex, true-grit—but the silly gadgets of civilization aside, we have plenty of reason to take pride in how we've matured. With survival now on the back burner, we've begun to reason—and it's about time—that we have a responsibility to protect, no longer just conquer, our wild places: that they, not we, are at risk. So please, do what you can. The following section will help you understand better what it means to "do what you can" while still making the most of your hiking experience. Anyone can take a hike, but hiking safely and well is an art requiring preparation and proper equipment.

Trail Etiquette

Zero impact. Always leave an area just like you found it—if not better than you found it. Avoid camping in fragile, alpine meadows and along the banks of streams and lakes. Use a camp stove versus building a wood fire. Pack up all of your trash and extra food. Bury human waste at least 100 feet from water sources under 6 to 8 inches of topsoil. Don't bathe with soap in a lake or stream—use prepackaged moistened towels to wipe off sweat and dirt, or bathe in the water without soap.

Stay on the trail. It's true, a path anywhere leads nowhere new, but purists will just have to get over it. Paths serve an important purpose; they limit impact on natural areas. Straying from a designated trail may seem innocent but it can cause damage to sensitive areas—damage that may take years to recover, if it can recover at all. Even simple shortcuts can be destructive. So, please, stay on the trail.

Leave no weeds. Noxious weeds tend to overtake other plants, which in turn affects animals and birds that depend on them for food. To minimize the spread of noxious weeds, hikers should regularly clean their boots, tents, packs, and hiking poles of mud and seeds. Also brush your dog to remove any weed seeds before heading off into a new area.

Keep your dog under control. You can buy a flexi-lead that allows your dog to go exploring along the trail, while allowing you the ability to reel him in should another hiker approach or should he decide to chase a rabbit. Always obey leash laws and be sure to bury your dog's waste or pack it in resealable plastic bags.

Respect other trail users. Often you're not the only one on the trail. With the rise in popularity of multiuse trails, you'll have to learn a new kind of respect, beyond the nod and "hello" approach you may be used to. First investigate whether you're on a multiuse trail, and assume the appropriate precautions. When you encounter motorized vehicles (ATVs, motorcycles, and 4WDs), be alert. Though they should always yield to the hiker, often they're going too fast or are too lost in the buzz of their engine to react to your presence. If you hear activity ahead, step off the trail just to be safe. Note that you're not likely to hear a mountain biker coming, so be prepared and know ahead of time whether you share the trail with them. Cyclists should always yield to hikers, but that's little comfort to the hiker. Be aware. When you approach horses or pack animals on the trail, always step quietly off the trail, preferably on the downhill side, and let them pass. If you're wearing a large backpack, it's often a good idea to sit down. To some animals, a hiker wearing a large backpack might appear threatening. Many national forests allow domesticated grazing, usually for sheep and cattle. Make sure your dog doesn't harass these animals, and respect ranchers' rights while you're enjoying yours.

Getting into Shape

Unless you want to be sore—and possibly have to shorten your trip or vacation—be sure to get in shape before a big hike. If you're terribly out of shape, start a walking program early, preferably eight weeks in advance. Start with a fifteen-minute walk during your lunch hour or after work and gradually increase your walking time to an hour. You should also increase your elevation gain. Walking briskly up hills really strengthens your leg muscles and gets your heart rate up. If you work in a storied office building, take the stairs instead of the elevator. If you prefer going to a gym, walk the treadmill or use a stair machine. You can further increase your strength and endurance by walking with a loaded backpack. Stationary exercises you might consider are squats, leg lifts, sit-ups, and push-ups. Other good ways to get in shape include biking, running, aerobics, and, of course, short hikes. Stretching before and after a hike keeps muscles flexible and helps avoid injuries.

Preparedness

It's been said that failing to plan means planning to fail. So do take the necessary time to plan your trip. Whether going on a short day hike or an extended backpack trip, always prepare for the worst. Simply remembering to pack a copy of the U.S. Army Survival Manual is not preparedness. Although it's not a bad idea if you plan on entering truly wild places, it's merely the tourniquet answer to a problem. You need to do your best to prevent the problem from arising in the first place. In order to survive—and to stay reasonably comfortable—you need to concern yourself with the basics: water, food, and shelter. Don't go on a hike without having these bases covered. And don't go on a hike expecting to find these items in the woods.

Water. Even in frigid conditions, you need at least two quarts of water a day to function efficiently. Add heat and taxing terrain and you can bump that figure up to one gallon. That's simply a base to work from—your metabolism and your level of conditioning can raise or lower that amount. Unless you know your level, assume that you need one gallon of water a day. Now, where do you plan on getting the water?

Preferably not from natural water sources. These sources can be loaded with intestinal disturbers, such as bacteria, viruses, and fertilizers. Giardia lamblia, the most common of these disturbers, is a protozoan parasite that lives part of its life cycle as a cyst in water sources. The parasite spreads when mammals defecate in water sources. Once ingested, Giardia can induce cramping, diarrhea, vomiting, and fatigue within two days to two weeks after ingestion. Giardiasis is treatable with prescription drugs. If you believe you've contracted giardiasis, see a doctor immediately.

Treating water. The best and easiest solution to avoid polluted water is to carry your water with you. Yet, depending on the nature of your hike and the duration, this may not be an option—one gallon of water weighs eight-and-a-half pounds. In that case, you'll need to look into treating water. Regardless of which method you choose, you should always carry some water with you in case of an emergency. Save this reserve until you absolutely need it.

There are three methods of treating water: boiling, chemical treatment, and filtering. If you boil water, it's recommended that you do so for ten to fifteen minutes. This is often impractical because you're forced to exhaust a great deal of your fuel supply. You can opt for chemical treatment, which will kill Giardia but will not take care of other chemical pollutants. Another drawback to chemical treatments is the unpleasant taste of the water after it's treated. You can remedy this by adding powdered drink mix to the water. Filters are the preferred method for treating water. Many filters remove Giardia, organic and inorganic contaminants, and don't leave an aftertaste. Water filters are far from perfect as they can easily become clogged or leak if a gasket wears out. It's always a good idea to carry a backup supply of chemical treatment tablets in case your filter decides to quit on you.

Food. If we're talking about survival, you can go days without food, as long as you have water. But we're also talking about comfort. Try to avoid foods that are high in sugar and fat like candy bars and potato chips. These food types are harder to digest and are low in nutritional value. Instead, bring along foods that are easy to pack, nutritious, and high in energy (e.g., bagels, nutrition bars, dehydrated fruit, gorp, and jerky). If you are on an overnight trip, easy-to-fix dinners include rice mixes with dehydrated potatoes, corn, pasta with cheese sauce, and soup mixes. For a tasty breakfast, you can fix hot oatmeal with brown sugar and reconstituted milk powder topped off with banana chips. If you like a hot drink in the morning, bring along herbal tea bags or hot chocolate. If you are a coffee junkie, you can purchase coffee that is packaged like tea bags. You can prepackage all of your meals in heavy-duty resealable plastic bags to keep food from spilling in your pack. These bags can be reused to pack out trash.

Shelter. The type of shelter you choose depends less on the conditions than on your tolerance for discomfort. Shelter comes in many forms—tent, tarp, lean-to, bivy sack, cabin, cave, etc. If you're camping in the desert, a bivy sack may suffice, but if you're above the treeline and a storm is approaching, a better choice is a three- or four-season tent. Tents are the logical and most popular choice for most backpackers as they're lightweight and packable—and you can rest assured that you always have shelter from the elements. Before you leave on your trip, anticipate what the weather and terrain will be like and plan for the type of shelter that will work best for your comfort level (see Equipment later in this section).

Finding a campsite. If there are established campsites, stick to those. If not, start looking for a campsite early—around 3:30 or 4:00 p.m. Stop at the first decent site you see. Depending on the area, it could be a long time before you find another suitable location. Pitch your camp in an area that's level. Make sure the area is at least 200 feet from fragile areas like lakeshores, meadows, and stream banks. And try to avoid areas thick in underbrush, as they can harbor insects and provide cover for approaching animals.

If you are camping in stormy, rainy weather, look for a rock outcrop or a shelter in the trees to keep the wind from blowing your tent all night. Be sure that you don't camp under trees with dead limbs that might break off on top of you. Also, try to find an area that has an absorbent surface, such as sandy soil or forest duff. This, in addition to camping on a surface with a slight angle, will provide better drainage. By all means, don't dig trenches to provide drainage around your tent—remember you're practicing zero-impact camping.

If you're in bear country, steer clear of creekbeds or animal paths. If you see any signs of a bear's presence (i.e., scat, footprints), relocate. You'll need to find a campsite near a tall tree where you can hang your food and other items that may attract bears such as deodorant, toothpaste, or soap. Carry a lightweight nylon rope with which to hang your food. As a rule, you should hang your food at least 20 feet from the ground and 5 feet away from the tree trunk. You can put food and other items in a waterproof stuff sack and tie one end of the rope to the stuff sack. To get the other end of the rope over the tree branch, tie a good size rock to it, and gently toss the rock over the tree branch. Pull the stuff sack up until it reaches the top of the branch and tie it off securely. Don't hang your food near your tent! If possible, hang your food at least 100 feet away from your campsite. Alternatives to hanging your food are bear-proof plastic tubes and metal bear boxes.

Lastly, think of comfort. Lie down on the ground where you intend to sleep and see if it's a good fit. For morning warmth (and a nice view to wake up to), have your tent face east.

First Aid

I know you're tough, but get 10 miles into the woods and develop a blister and you'll wish you had carried that first-aid kit. Face it, it's just plain good sense. Many companies produce lightweight, compact first-aid kits. Just make sure yours contains at least the following:

- Band–Aids
- mole skin
- various sterile gauze and dressings
- white surgical tape
- an Ace bandage
- an antihistamine
- aspirin
- Betadine solution
- a first–aid book
- Tums

- tweezers
- scissors
- antibacterial wipes
- triple-antibiotic ointment
- plastic gloves
- sterile cotton tip applicators
- syrup of ipecac (to induce vomiting)
- thermometer
- wire splint

Here are a few tips for dealing with and hopefully preventing certain ailments.

Sunburn. Take along sunscreen or sun block, protective clothing, and a wide-brimmed hat. If you do get a sunburn, treat the area with aloe vera gel, and protect the area from further sun exposure. At higher elevations, the sun's radiation can be particularly damaging to skin. Remember that your eyes are vulnerable to this radiation as well. Sunglasses can be a good way to prevent headaches and permanent eye damage from the sun, especially in places where light-colored rock or patches of snow reflect light up in your face.

Blisters. Be prepared to take care of these hike-spoilers by carrying moleskin (a lightly padded adhesive), gauze and tape, or adhesive bandages. An effective way to apply moleskin is to cut out a circle of moleskin and remove the center—like a doughnut—and place it over the blistered area. Cutting the center out will reduce the pressure applied to the sensitive skin. Other products can help you combat blisters. Some are applied to suspicious hot spots before a blister forms to help decrease friction to that area, while others are applied to the blister after it has popped to help prevent further irritation.

Insect bites and stings. You can treat most insect bites and stings by applying hydrocortisone 1% cream topically and taking a pain medication such as ibuprofen or acetaminophen to reduce swelling. If you forgot to pack these items, a cold compress or a paste of mud and ashes can sometimes assuage the itching and discomfort. Remove any stingers by using tweezers or scraping the area with your fingernail or a knife blade. Don't pinch the area as you'll only spread the venom.

Some hikers are highly sensitive to bites and stings and may have a serious allergic reaction that can be life threatening. Symptoms of a serious allergic reaction can include wheezing, an asthmatic attack, and shock. The treatment for this severe type of reaction is epinephrine. If you know that you are sensitive to bites and stings, carry a pre-packaged kit of epinephrine, which can be obtained only by prescription from your doctor.

Ticks. Ticks can carry diseases such as Rocky Mountain spotted fever and Lyme disease. The best defense is, of course, prevention. If you know you're going to be hiking through an area littered with ticks, wear long pants and a long sleeved shirt. You can apply a permethrin repellent to your clothing and a Deet repellent to exposed skin. At the end of your hike, do a spot check for ticks (and insects in general). If you do find a tick, coat the insect with petroleum jelly or tree sap to cut off its air supply. The tick should release its hold, but if it doesn't, grab the head of the tick firmly—with a pair of tweezers if you have them—and gently pull it away from the skin with a twisting motion. Sometimes the mouth parts linger, embedded in your skin. If this happens, try to remove them with a disinfected needle. Clean the affected area with an antibacterial cleanser and then apply triple antibiotic ointment. Monitor the area for a few days. If irritation persists or a white spot develops, see a doctor for possible infection.

Poison ivy, oak, and sumac. These skin irritants can be found most anywhere in North America and come in the form of a bush or a vine, having leaflets in groups of three, five, seven, or nine. Learn how to spot the plants. The oil they secrete can cause an allergic reaction in the form of blisters, usually about twelve hours after exposure. The itchy rash can last from ten days to several weeks. The best defense against these irritants is to wear clothing that covers the arms, legs and torso. For summer, zip-off cargo pants come in handy. There are also nonprescription lotions you can apply to exposed skin that guard against the effects of poison ivy/oak/sumac and can be washed off with soap and water. If you think you were in contact with the plants, after hiking (or even on the trail during longer hikes) wash with soap and water. Taking a hot shower with soap after you return home from your hike will also help to remove any lingering oil from your skin. Should you contract a rash from any of these plants, use an antihistamine to reduce the itching. If the rash is localized, create a light bleach/water wash to dry up the area. If the rash has spread, either tough it out or see your doctor about getting a dose of cortisone (available both orally and by injection).

Snakebites. Snakebites are rare in North America. Unless startled or provoked, the majority of snakes will not bite. If you are wise to their habitats and keep a careful eye on the trail, you should be just fine. When stepping over logs, first step on the log, making sure you can see what's on the other side before stepping down. Though your chances of being struck are slim, it's wise to know what to do in the event you are.

If a nonpoisonous snake bites you, allow the wound to bleed a small amount and then cleanse the wounded area with a Betadine solution (10% povidone iodine). Rinse the wound with clean water (preferably) or fresh urine (it might sound ugly, but it's sterile). Once the area is clean, cover it with triple antibiotic ointment and a clean bandage. Remember, most residual damage from snakebites, poisonous or otherwise, comes from infection, not the snake's venom. Keep the area as clean as possible and get medical attention immediately.

If you are bitten by a poisonous snake, remove the toxin with a suctioning device, found in a snakebite kit. If you do not have such a device, squeeze the wound—DO

NOT use your mouth for suction, as the venom will enter your bloodstream through the vessels under the tongue and head straight for your heart. Then, clean the wound just as you would a nonpoisonous bite. Tie a clean band of cloth snuggly around the afflicted appendage, about an inch or so above the bite (or the rim of the swelling). This is NOT a tourniquet—you want to simply slow the blood flow, not cut it off. Loosen the band if numbness ensues. Remove the band for a minute and reapply a little higher every ten minutes.

If it is your friend who's been bitten, treat him or her for shock—make the person comfortable, have him or her lie down, elevate the legs, and keep him or her warm. Avoid applying anything cold to the bite wound. Immobilize the affected area and remove any constricting items such as rings, watches, or restrictive clothing—swelling may occur. Once your friend is stable and relatively calm, hike out to get help. The victim should get treatment within twelve hours, ideally, which usually consists of a tetanus shot, antivenin, and antibiotics.

If you are alone and struck by a poisonous snake, stay calm. Hysteria will only quicken the venom's spread. Follow the procedure above, and do your best to reach help. When hiking out, don't run—you'll only increase the flow of blood throughout your system. Instead, walk calmly.

Dehydration. Have you ever hiked in hot weather and had a roaring headache and felt fatigued after only a few miles? More than likely you were dehydrated. Symptoms of dehydration include fatigue, headache, and decreased coordination and judgment. When you are hiking, your body's rate of fluid loss depends on the outside temperature, humidity, altitude, and your activity level. On average, a hiker walking in warm weather will lose four liters of fluid a day. That fluid loss is easily replaced by normal consumption of liquids and food. However, if a hiker is walking briskly in hot, dry weather and hauling a heavy pack, he or she can lose one to three liters of water an hour. It's important to always carry plenty of water and to stop often and drink fluids regularly, even if you aren't thirsty.

Heat exhaustion is the result of a loss of large amounts of electrolytes and often occurs if a hiker is dehydrated and has been under heavy exertion. Common symptoms of heat exhaustion include cramping, exhaustion, fatigue, lightheadedness, and nausea. You can treat heat exhaustion by getting out of the sun and drinking an electrolyte solution made up of one teaspoon of salt and one tablespoon of sugar dissolved in a liter of water. Drink this solution slowly over a period of one hour. Drinking plenty of fluids (preferably an electrolyte solution/sports drink) can prevent heat exhaustion. Avoid hiking during the hottest parts of the day, and wear breathable clothing, a wide-brimmed hat, and sunglasses.

Hypothermia is one of the biggest dangers in the backcountry, especially for day hikers in the summertime. That may sound strange, but imagine starting out on a hike in midsummer when it's sunny and 80 degrees out. You're clad in nylon shorts and a cotton T-shirt. About halfway through your hike, the sky begins to cloud up, and in the next hour a light drizzle begins to fall and the wind starts to pick up. Before you know it, you are soaking wet and shivering—the perfect recipe for hypothermia. More advanced signs include decreased coordination, slurred speech, and blurred vision. When a victim's temperature falls below 92 degrees, the blood pressure and pulse plummet, possibly leading to coma and death.

To avoid hypothermia, always bring a windproof/rainproof shell, a fleece jacket, tights made of a breathable, synthetic fiber, gloves, and hat when you are hiking in the mountains. Learn to adjust your clothing layers based on the temperature. If you are climbing uphill at a moderate pace you will stay warm, but when you stop for a break you'll become cold quickly, unless you add more layers of clothing.

If a hiker is showing advanced signs of hypothermia, dress him or her in dry clothes and make sure he or she is wearing a hat and gloves. Place the person in a sleeping bag in a tent or shelter that will protect him or her from the wind and other elements. Give the person warm fluids to drink and keep him awake.

Frostbite. When the mercury dips below 32 degrees, your extremities begin to chill. If a persistent chill attacks a localized area, say, your hands or your toes, the circulatory system reacts by cutting off blood flow to the affected area—the idea being to protect and preserve the body's overall temperature. And so it's death by attrition for the affected area. Ice crystals start to form from the water in the cells of the neglected tissue. Deprived of heat, nourishment, and now water, the tissue literally starves. This is frostbite.

Prevention is your best defense against this situation. Most prone to frostbite are your face, hands, and feet, so protect these areas well. Wool is the material of choice because it provides ample air space for insulation and draws moisture away from the skin. Synthetic fabrics, however, have recently made great strides in the cold weather clothing market. Do your research. A pair of light silk liners under your regular gloves is a good trick for keeping warm. They afford some additional warmth, but more importantly they'll allow you to remove your mitts for tedious work without exposing the skin.

If your feet or hands start to feel cold or numb due to the elements, warm them as quickly as possible. Place cold hands under your armpits or bury them in your crotch. If your feet are cold, change your socks. If there's plenty of room in your boots, add another pair of socks. Do remember, though, that constricting your feet in tight boots can restrict blood flow and actually make your feet colder more quickly. Your socks need to have breathing room if they're going to be effective. Dead air provides insulation. If your face is cold, place your warm hands over your face, or simply wear a head stocking.

Should your skin go numb and start to appear white and waxy, chances are you've got or are developing frostbite. Don't try to thaw the area unless you can maintain the warmth. In other words, don't stop to warm up your frostbitten feet only to head back on the trail. You'll do more damage than good. Tests have shown that hikers who walked on thawed feet did more harm, and endured more pain, than hikers who left the affected areas alone. Do your best to get out of the cold entirely and seek medical attention—which usually consists of performing a rapid rewarming in water for twenty to thirty minutes.

The overall objective in preventing both hypothermia and frostbite is to keep the body's core warm. Protect key areas where heat escapes, like the top of the head, and maintain the proper nutrition level. Foods that are high in calories aid the body in producing heat. Never smoke or drink when you're in situations where the cold is threatening. By affecting blood flow, these activities ultimately cool the body's core temperature.

Altitude sickness (AMS). High lofty peaks, clear alpine lakes, and vast mountain views beckon hikers to the high country. But those who like to venture high may become victims of altitude sickness (also known as Acute Mountain Sickness—AMS). Altitude sickness is your body's reaction to insufficient oxygen in the blood due to decreased barometric pressure. While some hikers may feel lightheaded, nauseous, and experience shortness of breath at 7,000 feet, others may not experience these symptoms until they reach 10,000 feet or higher.

Slowing your ascent to high places and giving your body a chance to acclimatize to the higher elevations can prevent altitude sickness. For example, if you live at sea level and are planning a weeklong backpacking trip to elevations between 7,000 and 12,000 feet, start by staying below 7,000 feet for one night, then move to between 7,000 and 10,000 feet for another night or two. Avoid strenuous exertion and alcohol to give your body a chance to adjust to the new altitude. It's also important to eat light food and drink plenty of nonalcoholic fluids, preferably water. Loss of appetite at altitude is common, but you must eat!

Most hikers who experience mild to moderate AMS develop a headache and/or nausea, grow lethargic, and have problems sleeping. The treatment for AMS is simple: stop heading uphill. Keep eating and drinking water and take meds for the headache. You actually need to take more breaths at altitude than at sea level, so breathe a little faster without hyperventilating. If symptoms don't improve over twenty-four to forty-eight hours, descend. Once a victim descends about 2,000 to 3,000 feet, his signs will usually begin to diminish.

Severe AMS comes in two forms: High Altitude Pulmonary Edema (HAPE) and High Altitude Cerebral Edema (HACE). HAPE, an accumulation of fluid in the lungs, can occur above 8,000 feet. Symptoms include rapid heart rate, shortness of breath at rest, AMS symptoms, dry cough developing into a wet cough, gurgling sounds, flu-like or bronchitis symptoms, and lack of muscle coordination. HAPE is life threatening so descend immediately, at least 2,000 to 4,000 feet. HACE usually occurs above 12,000 feet but sometimes occurs above 10,000 feet. Symptoms are similar to HAPE but also include seizures, hallucinations, paralysis, and vision disturbances. Descend immediately—HACE is also life threatening.

Hantavirus Pulmonary Syndrome (HPS). Deer mice spread the virus that causes HPS, and humans contract it from breathing it in, usually when they've disturbed an area with dust and mice feces from nests or surfaces with mice droppings or urine.

Exposure to large numbers of rodents and their feces or urine presents the greatest risk. As hikers, we sometimes enter old buildings, and often deer mice live in these places. We may not be around long enough to be exposed, but do be aware of this disease. About half the people who develop HPS die. Symptoms are flu-like and appear about two to three weeks after exposure. After initial symptoms, a dry cough and shortness of breath follow. Breathing is difficult. If you even think you might have HPS, see a doctor immediately!

Natural Hazards

Besides tripping over a rock or tree root on the trail, there are some real hazards to be aware of while hiking. Even if where you're hiking doesn't have the plethora of poisonous snakes and plants, insects, and grizzly bears found in other parts of the United States, there are a few weather conditions and predators you may need to take into account.

Lightning. Thunderstorms build over the mountains almost every day during the summer. Lightning is generated by thunderheads and can strike without warning, even several miles away from the nearest overhead cloud. The best rule of thumb is to start leaving exposed peaks, ridges, and canyon rims by about noon. This time can vary a little depending on storm buildup. Keep an eye on cloud formation and don't underestimate how fast a storm can build. The bigger they get, the more likely a thunderstorm will happen. Lightning takes the path of least resistance, so if you're the high point, it might choose you. Ducking under a rock overhang is dangerous as you form the shortest path between the rock and ground. If you dash below treeline, avoid standing under the only or the tallest tree. If you are caught above treeline, stay away from anything metal you might be carrying. Move down off the ridge slightly to a low, treeless point and squat until the storm passes. If you have an insulating pad, squat on it. Avoid having both your hands and feet touching the ground at once and never lay flat. If you hear a buzzing sound or feel your hair standing on end, move quickly as an electrical charge is building up.

Flash floods. On July 31, 1976, a torrential downpour unleashed by a thunderstorm dumped tons of water into the Big Thompson watershed near Estes Park, Colorado. Within hours, a wall of water moved down the narrow canyon killing 139 people and causing more than $30 million in property damage. The spooky thing about flash floods, especially in western canyons, is that they can appear out of nowhere from a storm many miles away. While hiking or driving in canyons, keep an eye on the weather. Always climb to safety if danger threatens. Flash floods usually subside quickly, so be patient and don't cross a swollen stream.

Bears. Most of the United States (outside of the Pacific Northwest and parts of the Northern Rockies) does not have a grizzly bear population, although some rumors exist about sightings where there should be none. Black bears are plentiful, however. Here are some tips in case you and a bear scare each other. Most of all, avoid scaring a bear. Watch for bear tracks (five toes) and droppings (sizable with leaves, partly digested berries, seeds, and/or animal fur). Talk or sing where visibility or hearing are limited. Keep a clean camp, hang food, and don't sleep in the clothes you wore while cooking. Be especially careful in spring to avoid getting between a mother and her cubs. In late summer and fall bears are busy eating berries and acorns to fatten up for winter, so be extra careful around berry bushes and oakbrush. If you do encounter a bear, move away slowly while facing the bear, talk softly, and avoid direct eye contact. Give the bear room to escape. Since bears are very curious, it might stand upright to get a better whiff of you, and it may even charge you to try to intimidate you. Try to stay calm. If a bear does attack you, fight back with anything you have handy. Unleashed dogs have been known to come running back to their owners with a bear close behind. Keep your dog on a leash or leave it at home.

Mountain lions. Mountain lions appear to be getting more comfortable around humans as long as deer (their favorite prey) are in an area with adequate cover. Usually elusive and quiet, lions rarely attack people. If you meet a lion, give it a chance to escape. Stay calm and talk firmly to it. Back away slowly while facing the lion. If you run, you'll only encourage the curious cat to chase you. Make yourself look large by opening a jacket, if you have one, or waving your hiking poles. If the lion behaves aggressively throw stones, sticks, or whatever you can while remaining tall. If a lion does attack, fight for your life with anything you can grab.

Moose. Because moose have very few natural predators, they don't fear humans like other animals. You might find moose in sagebrush and wetter areas of willow, aspen, and pine, or in beaver habitats. Mothers with calves, as well as bulls during mating season, can be particularly aggressive. If a moose threatens you, back away slowly and talk calmly to it. Keep your pets away from moose.

Other considerations. Hunting is a popular sport in the United States, especially during rifle season in October and November. Hiking is still enjoyable in those months in many areas, so just take a few precautions. First, learn when the different hunting seasons start and end in the area in which you'll be hiking. During this time frame, be sure to wear at least a blaze orange hat, and possibly put an orange vest over your pack. Don't be surprised to see hunters in camo outfits carrying bows or muzzleloading rifles around during their season. If you would feel more comfortable without hunters around, hike in national parks and monuments or state and local parks where hunting is not allowed.

Navigation

Whether you are going on a short hike in a familiar area or planning a weeklong backpack trip, you should always be equipped with the proper navigational equipment—at the very least a detailed map and a sturdy compass.

Maps. There are many different types of maps available to help you find your way on the trail. Easiest to find are Forest Service maps and BLM (Bureau of Land Management) maps. These maps tend to cover large areas, so be sure they are detailed enough for your particular trip. You can also obtain National Park maps as well as high quality maps from private companies and trail groups. These maps can be obtained either from outdoor stores or ranger stations.

U.S. Geological Survey topographic maps are particularly popular with hikers—especially serious backcountry hikers. These maps contain the standard map symbols such as roads, lakes, and rivers, as well as contour lines that show the details of the trail terrain like ridges, valleys, passes, and mountain peaks. The 7.5-minute series (1 inch on the map equals approximately ⅖ mile on the ground) provides the closest inspection available. USGS maps are available by mail (U.S. Geological Survey, Map Distribution Branch, P.O. Box 25286, Denver, CO 80225), or at mapping.usgs.gov/esic/to_order.html.

If you want to check out the high-tech world of maps, you can purchase topographic maps on CD-ROM. These software-mapping programs let you select a route on your computer, print it out, then take it with you on the trail. Some software mapping programs let you insert symbols and labels, download waypoints from a GPS unit, and export the maps to other software programs.

The art of map reading is a skill that you can develop by first practicing in an area you are familiar with. To begin, orient the map so the map is lined up in the correct direction (i.e. north on the map is lined up with true north). Next, familiarize yourself with the map symbols and try and match them up with terrain features around you such as a high ridge, mountain peak, river, or lake. If you are practicing with a USGS map, notice the contour lines. On gentler terrain these contour lines are spaced further apart, and on steeper terrain they are closer together. Pick a short loop trail, and stop frequently to check your position on the map. As you practice map reading, you'll learn how to anticipate a steep section on the trail or a good place to take a rest break, and so on.

Compasses. First off, the sun is not a substitute for a compass. So, what kind of compass should you have? Here are some characteristics you should look for: a rectangular base with detailed scales, a liquid-filled housing, protective housing, a sighting line on the mirror, luminous alignment and back-bearing arrows, a luminous north-seeking arrow, and a well-defined bezel ring.

You can learn compass basics by reading the detailed instructions included with your compass. If you want to fine-tune your compass skills, sign up for an orienteering class or purchase a book on compass reading. Once you've learned the basic skills of using a compass, remember to practice these skills before you head into the backcountry.

If you are a klutz at using a compass, you may be interested in checking out the technical wizardry of the GPS (Global Positioning System) device. The GPS was developed by the Pentagon and works off twenty-four NAVSTAR satellites, which were designed to guide missiles to their targets. A GPS device is a handheld unit that calculates your latitude and longitude with the easy press of a button. The Department of Defense used to scramble the satellite signals a bit to prevent civilians (and spies!)

from getting extremely accurate readings, but that practice was discontinued in May 2000, and GPS units now provide nearly pinpoint accuracy (within 30 to 60 feet).

There are many different types of GPS units available and they range in price from $100 to $400. In general, all GPS units have a display screen and keypad where you input information. In addition to acting as a compass, the unit allows you to plot your route, easily retrace your path, track your travelling speed, find the mileage between waypoints, and calculate the total mileage of your route.

Before you purchase a GPS unit, keep in mind that these devices don't pick up signals indoors, in heavily wooded areas, or in ravines, or in deep valleys.

Pedometers. A pedometer is a small, clip-on unit with a digital display that calculates your hiking distance in miles or kilometers based on your walking stride. Some units also calculate the calories you burn and your total hiking time. Pedometers are available at most large outdoor stores and range in price from $20 to $40.

Trip Planning

Planning your hiking adventure begins with letting a friend or relative know your trip itinerary so they can call for help if you don't return at your scheduled time. Your next task is to make sure you are outfitted to experience the risks and rewards of the trail. This section highlights gear and clothing you may want to take with you to get the most out of your hike.

Day Hikes
- camera/film
- compass/GPS unit
- pedometer
- daypack
- first-aid kit
- food
- guidebook
- headlamp/flashlight with extra batteries and bulbs
- hat
- insect repellant
- knife/multipurpose tool
- map
- matches in waterproof container and fire starter
- Polar Fleece jacket
- raingear
- space blanket
- sunglasses
- sunscreen
- swimsuit
- watch
- water
- water bottles/water hydration system

Overnight Trip

- backpack and waterproof rain cover
- backpacker's trowel
- bandanna
- bear repellant spray
- bear bell
- biodegradable soap
- pot scrubber
- collapsible water container (2–3 gallon capacity)
- clothing—extra wool socks, shirt and shorts
- cook set/utensils
- ditty bags to store gear
- extra plastic resealable bags
- gaiters
- garbage bag
- ground cloth
- journal/pen
- nylon rope to hang food
- long underwear
- permit (if required)
- rain jacket and pants
- sandals to wear around camp and to ford streams
- sleeping bag
- waterproof stuff sack
- sleeping pad
- small bath towel
- stove and fuel
- tent
- toiletry items
- water filter
- whistle

Equipment

With the outdoor market currently flooded with products, many of which are pure gimmickry, it seems impossible to both differentiate and choose. Do I really need a tropical-fish-lined collapsible shower? (No, you don't.) The only defense against the maddening quantity of items thrust in your face is to think practically—and to do so before you go shopping. The worst buys are impulsive buys. Since most name brands will differ only slightly in quality, it's best to know what you're looking for in terms of function. Buy only what you need. You will, don't forget, be carrying what you've bought on your back. Here are some things to keep in mind before you go shopping.

Clothes. Clothing is your armor against Mother Nature's little surprises. Hikers should be prepared for any possibility, especially when hiking in mountainous areas. Adequate rain protection and extra layers of clothing are a good idea. In summer, a wide-brimmed hat can help keep the sun at bay. In the winter months the first layer you'll want to wear is a "wicking" layer of long underwear that keeps perspiration away from your skin. Wear long underwear made from synthetic fibers that wick moisture away from the skin and draw it toward the next layer of clothing, where it then evaporates. Avoid wearing long underwear made of cotton as it is slow to dry and keeps moisture next to your skin.

The second layer you'll wear is the "insulating" layer. Aside from keeping you warm, this layer needs to "breathe" so you stay dry while hiking. A fabric that provides insulation and dries quickly is fleece. It's interesting to note that this one-of-a-kind fabric is made out of recycled plastic. Purchasing a zip-up jacket made of this material is highly recommended.

The last line of layering defense is the "shell" layer. You'll need some type of waterproof, windproof, breathable jacket that will fit over all of your other layers. It should have a large hood that fits over a hat. You'll also need a good pair of rain pants made from a similar waterproof, breathable fabric. Some Gore-Tex jackets cost as much as $500, but you should know that there are more affordable fabrics out there that work just as well.

Now that you've learned the basics of layering, you can't forget to protect your hands and face. In cold, windy, or rainy weather you'll need a hat made of wool or fleece and insulated, waterproof gloves that will keep your hands warm and toasty. As mentioned earlier, buying an additional pair of light silk liners to wear under your regular gloves is a good idea.

Footwear. If you have any extra money to spend on your trip, put that money into boots or trail shoes. Poor shoes will bring a hike to a halt faster than anything else. To avoid this annoyance, buy shoes that provide support and are lightweight and flexible. A lightweight hiking boot is better than a heavy, leather mountaineering boot for most day hikes and backpacking. Trail running shoes provide a little extra cushion and are made in a high-top style that many people wear for hiking. These running shoes are lighter, more flexible, and more breathable than hiking boots. If you know you'll be hiking in wet weather often, purchase boots or shoes with a Gore-Tex liner, which will help keep your feet dry.

When buying your boots, be sure to wear the same type of socks you'll be wearing on the trail. If the boots you're buying are for cold weather hiking, try the boots on while wearing two pairs of socks. Speaking of socks, a good cold weather sock combination is to wear a thinner sock made of wool or polypropylene covered by a heavier outer sock made of wool. The inner sock protects the foot from the rubbing effects of the outer sock and prevents blisters. Many outdoor stores have some type of ramp to simulate hiking uphill and downhill. Be sure to take advantage of this test, as toe-jamming boot fronts can be very painful and debilitating on the downhill trek.

Once you've purchased your footwear, be sure to break them in before you hit the trail. New footwear is often stiff and needs to be stretched and molded to your foot.

Hiking poles. Hiking poles help with balance, and more importantly take pressure off your knees. The ones with shock absorbers are easier on your elbows and knees. Some poles even come with a camera attachment to be used as a monopod. And heaven forbid you meet a mountain lion, bear, or unfriendly dog, the poles can make you look a lot bigger.

Backpacks. No matter what type of hiking you do you'll need a pack of some sort to carry the basic trail essentials. There are a variety of backpacks on the market, but let's first discuss what you intend to use it for. Day hikes or overnight trips?

If you plan on doing a day hike, a daypack should have some of the following characteristics: a padded hip belt that's at least 2 inches in diameter (avoid packs with only a small nylon piece of webbing for a hip belt); a chest strap (the chest strap helps stabilize the pack against your body); external pockets to carry water and other items that you want easy access to; an internal pocket to hold keys, a knife, a wallet, and other miscellaneous items; an external lashing system to hold a jacket; and a hydration pocket for carrying a hydration system (which consists of a water bladder with an attachable drinking hose).

For short hikes, some hikers like to use a fanny pack to store just a camera, food, a compass, a map, and other trail essentials. Most fanny packs have pockets for two water bottles and a padded hip belt.

If you intend to do an extended, overnight trip, there are multiple considerations. First off, you need to decide what kind of framed pack you want. There are two backpack types for backpacking: the internal frame and the external frame. An internal frame pack rests closer to your body, making it more stable and easier to balance when hiking over rough terrain. An external frame pack is just that, an aluminum frame attached to the exterior of the pack. An external frame pack is better for long backpack trips because it distributes the pack weight better and you can carry heavier loads. It's easier to pack, and your gear is more accessible. It also offers better back ventilation in hot weather.

The most critical measurement for fitting a pack is torso length. The pack needs to rest evenly on your hips without sagging. A good pack will come in two or three sizes and have straps and hip belts that are adjustable according to your body size and characteristics.

When you purchase a backpack, go to an outdoor store with salespeople who are knowledgeable in how to properly fit a pack. Once the pack is fitted for you, load the pack with the amount of weight you plan on taking on the trail. The weight of the pack should be distributed evenly and you should be able to swing your arms and walk briskly without feeling out of balance. Another good technique for evaluating a pack is to walk up and down stairs and make quick turns to the right and to the left to be sure the pack doesn't feel out of balance. Other features that are nice to have on a backpack include a removable day pack or fanny pack, external pockets for extra water, and extra lash points to attach a jacket or other items.

Sleeping bags and pads. Sleeping bags are rated by temperature. You can purchase a bag made of synthetic fiber, or you can buy a goose down bag. Goose down bags are more expensive, but they have a higher insulating capacity by weight and will keep their loft longer. You'll want to purchase a bag with a temperature rating that fits the time of year and conditions you are most likely to camp in. One caveat: The techno-standard for temperature ratings is far from perfect. Ratings vary from manufacturer to manufacturer, so to protect yourself you should purchase a bag rated 10 to 15 degrees below the temperature you expect to be camping in. Synthetic bags are more resistant to water than down bags, but many down bags are now made with a Gore-Tex shell that helps to repel water. Down bags are also more compressible than synthetic bags and take up less room in your pack, which is an important consideration if you are planning a multiday backpack trip. Features to look for in a sleeping bag include a mummy style bag, a hood you can cinch down around your head in cold weather, and draft tubes along the zippers that help keep heat in and drafts out.

You'll also want a sleeping pad to provide insulation and padding from the cold ground. There are different types of sleeping pads available, from the more expensive self-inflating air mattresses to the less expensive closed-cell foam pads. Self-inflating air mattresses are usually heavier than closed-cell foam mattresses and are prone to punctures.

Tents. The tent is your home away from home while on the trail. It provides protection from wind, snow, rain, and insects. A three-season tent is a good choice for backpacking and can range in price from $100 to $500. These lightweight and versatile tents provide protection in all types of weather, except heavy snowstorms or high winds, and range in weight from four to eight pounds. Look for a tent that's easy to set up and will easily fit two people with gear. Dome type tents usually offer more headroom and places to store gear. Other tent designs include a vestibule where you can store wet boots and backpacks. Some nice-to-have items in a tent include interior pockets to store small items and lashing points to hang a clothesline. Most three-season tents come with stakes so you can secure the tent in high winds. Before you purchase a tent, set it up and take it down a few times to be sure it is easy to handle. Also, sit inside the tent and make sure it has enough room for you and your gear.

Cell phones. Many hikers are carrying their cell phones into the backcountry these days in case of emergency. That's fine and good, but please know that cell phone coverage is often poor to nonexistent in valleys, canyons, and thick forest. More importantly people have started to call for help because they're tired or lost. Let's go back to being prepared. You are responsible for yourself in the backcountry. Use your brain to avoid problems, and if you do encounter one, first use your brain to try to correct the situation. Only use your cell phone, if it works, in true emergencies.

Hiking with Children

Hiking with children isn't a matter of how many miles you can cover or how much elevation gain you make in a day; it's about seeing and experiencing nature through their eyes.

Kids like to explore and have fun. They like to stop and point out bugs and plants, look under rocks, jump in puddles, and throw sticks. If you're taking a toddler or young child on a hike, start with a trail that you're familiar with. Trails that have interesting things for kids, like piles of leaves to play in or a small stream to wade through during the summer, will make the hike much more enjoyable for them and will keep them from getting bored.

You can keep your child's attention if you have a strategy before starting on the trail. Using games is not only an effective way to keep a child's attention, it's also a great way to teach him or her about nature. Play hide and seek, where your child is the mouse and you are the hawk. Quiz children on the names of plants and animals. If your children are old enough, let them carry their own daypack filled with snacks and water. So that you are sure to go at their pace and not yours, let them lead the way. Playing follow the leader works particularly well when you have a group of children. Have each child take a turn at being the leader.

With children, a lot of clothing is key. The only thing predictable about weather is that it will change. Especially in mountainous areas, weather can change dramatically in a very short time. Always bring extra clothing for children, regardless of the season. In the winter, have your children wear wool socks, and warm layers such as long underwear, a fleece jacket and hat, wool mittens, and good rain gear. It's not a bad idea to have these along in late fall and early spring as well. Good footwear is also important. A sturdy pair of high top tennis shoes or lightweight hiking boots are the best bet for little ones. If you're hiking in the summer near a lake or stream, bring along a pair of old sneakers that your child can put on when he wants to go exploring in the water. Remember when you're near any type of water, always watch your child at all times. Also, keep a close eye on teething toddlers who may decide a rock or leaf of poison oak is an interesting item to put in their mouth.

From spring through fall, you'll want your kids to wear a wide-brimmed hat to keep their face, head, and ears protected from the hot sun. Also, make sure your children wear sunscreen at all times. Choose a brand without Paba—children have sensitive skin and may have an allergic reaction to sunscreen that contains Paba. If you are hiking with a child younger than six months, don't use sunscreen or insect repellent. Instead, be sure that their head, face, neck, and ears are protected from the sun with a wide-brimmed hat, and that all other skin exposed to the sun is protected with the appropriate clothing.

Remember that food is fun. Kids like snacks so it's important to bring a lot of munchies for the trail. Stopping often for snack breaks is a fun way to keep the trail interesting. Raisins, apples, granola bars, crackers and cheese, cereal, and trail mix all make great snacks. If your child is old enough to carry her own backpack, fill it with treats before you leave. If your kids don't like drinking water, you can bring boxes of fruit juice.

Avoid poorly designed child-carrying packs—you don't want to break your back carrying your child. Most child-carrying backpacks designed to hold a forty-pound child will contain a large carrying pocket to hold diapers and other items. Some have an optional rain/sun hood.

Hiking with Your Dog

Bringing your furry friend with you is always more fun than leaving him behind. Our canine pals make great trail buddies because they never complain and always make good company. Hiking with your dog can be a rewarding experience, especially if you plan ahead.

Getting your dog in shape. Before you plan outdoor adventures with your dog, make sure he's in shape for the trail. Getting your dog into shape takes the same discipline as getting yourself into shape, but luckily, your dog can get in shape with you. Take your dog with you on your daily runs or walks. If there is a park near your house, hit a tennis ball or play Frisbee with your dog.

Swimming is also an excellent way to get your dog into shape. If there is a lake or river near where you live and your dog likes the water, have him retrieve a tennis ball or stick. Gradually build your dog's stamina up over a two- to three-month period. A good rule of thumb is to assume that your dog will travel twice as far as you will on the trail. If you plan on doing a 5-mile hike, be sure your dog is in shape for a 10-mile hike.

Training your dog for the trail. Before you go on your first hiking adventure with your dog, be sure he has a firm grasp on the basics of canine etiquette and behavior. Make sure he can sit, lie down, stay, and come. One of the most important commands you can teach your canine pal is to "come" under any situation. It's easy for your friend's nose to lead him astray or possibly get lost. Another helpful command is the "get behind" command. When you're on a hiking trail that's narrow, you can have your dog follow behind you when other trail users approach. Nothing is more bothersome than an enthusiastic dog that runs back and forth on the trail and disrupts the peace of the trail for others. When you see other trail users approaching you on the trail, give them the right of way by quietly stepping off the trail and making your dog lie down and stay until they pass.

Equipment. The most critical pieces of equipment you can invest in for your dog are proper identification and a sturdy leash. Flexi-leads work well for hiking because they give your dog more freedom to explore but still leave you in control. Make sure your dog has identification that includes your name and address and a number for your veterinarian. Other forms of identification for your dog include a tattoo or a microchip. You should consult your veterinarian for more information on these last two options.

The next piece of equipment you'll want to consider is a pack for your dog. By no means should you hold all of your dog's essentials in your pack—let him carry his own gear! Dogs that are in good shape can carry 30 to 40 percent of their own weight.

Most packs are fitted by a dog's weight and girth measurement. Companies that make dog packs generally include guidelines to help you pick out the size that's right for your dog. Some characteristics to look for when purchasing a pack for your dog include a harness that contains two padded girth straps, a padded chest strap, leash attachments, removable saddle bags, internal water bladders, and external gear cords.

You can introduce your dog to the pack by first placing the empty pack on his back and letting him wear it around the yard. Keep an eye on him during this first introduction. He may decide to chew through the straps if you aren't watching him closely. Once he learns to treat the pack as an object of fun and not a foreign enemy, fill the pack evenly on both sides with a few ounces of dog food in resealable plastic bags. Have your dog wear his pack on your daily walks for a period of two to three weeks. Each week add a little more weight to the pack until your dog will accept carrying the maximum amount of weight he can carry.

You can also purchase collapsible water and dog food bowls for your dog. These bowls are lightweight and can easily be stashed into your pack or your dog's. If you are hiking on rocky terrain or in the snow, you can purchase footwear for your dog that will protect his feet from cuts and bruises.

Always carry plastic bags to remove feces from the trail. It is a courtesy to other trail users and helps protect local wildlife.

The following is a list of items to bring when you take your dog hiking: collapsible water bowls, a comb, a collar and a leash, dog food, plastic bags for feces, a dog pack, flea/tick powder, paw protection, water, and a first-aid kit that contains eye ointment, tweezers, scissors, stretchy foot wrap, gauze, antibacterial wash, sterile cotton tip applicators, antibiotic ointment, and cotton wrap.

First aid for your dog. Your dog is just as prone—if not more prone—to getting in trouble on the trail as you are, so be prepared. Here's a rundown of the more likely misfortunes that might befall your little friend.

Bees and wasps. If a bee or wasp stings your dog, remove the stinger with a pair of tweezers and place a mudpack or a cloth dipped in cold water over the affected area.

Porcupines. One good reason to keep your dog on a leash is to prevent it from getting a nose full of porcupine quills. You may be able to remove the quills with pliers, but a veterinarian is the best person to do this nasty job because most dogs need to be sedated.

Heat stroke. Avoid hiking with your dog in really hot weather. Dogs with heat stroke will pant excessively, lie down and refuse to get up, and become lethargic and disoriented. If your dog shows any of these signs on the trail, have him lie down in the shade. If you are near a stream, pour cool water over your dog's entire body to help bring his body temperature back to normal.

Heartworm. Dogs get heartworms from mosquitoes that carry the disease in the prime mosquito months of July and August. Giving your dog a monthly pill prescribed by your veterinarian easily prevents this condition.

Plant pitfalls. One of the biggest plant hazards for dogs on the trail is foxtails. Foxtails are pointed grass seed heads that bury themselves in your friend's fur, between his toes, and even get in his ear canal. If left unattended, these nasty seeds can work their way under the skin and cause abscesses and other problems. If you have a long-haired dog, consider trimming the hair between his toes and giving him a summer haircut to help prevent foxtails from attaching to his fur. After every hike, always look over your dog for these seeds—especially between his toes and his ears.

Other plant hazards include burrs, thorns, thistles, and poison oak. If you find any burrs or thistles on your dog, remove them as soon as possible before they become an unmanageable mat. Thorns can pierce a dog's foot and cause a great deal of pain. If you see that your dog is lame, stop and check his feet for thorns. Dogs are immune to poison oak but they can pick up the sticky, oily substance from the plant and transfer it to you.

Protect those paws. Be sure to keep your dog's nails trimmed so he avoids getting soft tissue or joint injuries. If your dog slows and refuses to go on, check to see that his paws aren't torn or worn. You can protect your dog's paws from trail hazards such as sharp gravel, foxtails, lava scree, and thorns by purchasing dog boots.

Sunburn. If your dog has light skin he is an easy target for sunburn on his nose and other exposed skin areas. You can apply a nontoxic sunscreen to exposed skin areas that will help protect him from overexposure to the sun.

Ticks and fleas. Ticks can easily give your dog Lyme disease, as well as other diseases. Before you hit the trail, treat your dog with a flea and tick spray or powder. You can also ask your veterinarian about a once-a-month pour-on treatment that repels fleas and ticks.

Mosquitoes and deer flies. These little flying machines can do a job on your dog's snout and ears. Best bet is to spray your dog with fly repellent for horses to discourage both pests.

Giardia. Dogs can get giardia, which results in diarrhea. It is usually not debilitating, but it's definitely messy. A vaccine against giardia is available.

Mushrooms. Make sure your dog doesn't sample mushrooms along the trail. They could be poisonous to him, but he doesn't know that.

When you are finally ready to hit the trail with your dog, keep in mind that national parks and many wilderness areas do not allow dogs on trails. Your best bet is to hike in national forests, BLM lands, and state parks. Always call ahead to see what the restrictions are.

Hike Index

About the Author

John L. Young was born and raised in Altoona, Pennsylvania. He has a degree in journalism and is a former newspaper reporter and columnist. His outdoor and travel articles have appeared in *Pennsylvania Magazine, Ohio Magazine,* and *Pursuits,* a publication of the Pennsylvania Tourism Office. His nonfiction books include *Unemployed No More, Murder at the Airport Inn, Murder in the Courtroom,* and *Hiking Pennsylvania.*